How to Run
A
FAMILY
BUSINESS

HOW TO RUN

A

FAMILY BUSINESS

How to own, operate
and ensure the
continuation of your
family business.

Michael Friedman & Scott Friedman

BETTERWAY BOOKS

Cincinnati, Ohio

97   96   95   94   93   5   4   3   2   1

Library of Congress Cataloging in Publication Data

Friedman, Michael H.
    How to run a family business / by Michael H. Friedman and Scott E.
Friedman. — 1st ed.
        p.   cm.
    Includes index.
    ISBN 1-55870-320-9
    1. Family-owned business enterprises — Management. I. Friedman, Scott E.
II. Title.
HD62.25.F748   1994
658.02'2 — dc20   93-41699
                                                                        CIP

Edited by Mary L. Sproles
Interior design by Brian Roeth

Quantity Discounts Available
This and other Betterway Books are available at a discount when purchased in bulk. Schools, organizations, corporations and others interested in purchasing bulk quantities of this book should contact the SPECIAL SALES DEPART-MENT of F&W Publications at 1-800-289-0963 (8 A.M.-5 P.M. Eastern Time) or write to this department at 1507 Dana Avenue, Cincinnati, OH 45207.

DISCLAIMER

This publication is designed to provide accurate and authoritative information regarding its subject matter. It is sold with the understanding that the publisher and authors are not engaged in rendering legal or other professional services and nothing contained in this book is to be considered as the rendering of legal advice for specific cases. If legal advice or other expert assistance is required, the services of a competent professional person should be sought. This book is intended for educational and informational purposes only. (From a declaration of principles jointly adopted by a committee of the American Bar Association and a committee of publishers.)

ABOUT THE AUTHORS

Michael H. Friedman

Michael H. Friedman is a partner in the commercial Department of Pepper, Hamilton & Scheetz, an international law firm headquartered in Philadelphia. He received a B.A. from Hamilton College, an M.A. from the University of Chicago, and a J.D. from the University of Virginia School of Law and is a member of Phi Beta Kappa and Order of the Coif. Mr. Friedman has previously published articles on securities regulation and is a past chair of the Mergers and Acquisitions Committee of the Philadelphia Bar Association's Business Section.

Scott E. Friedman

Scott E. Friedman is a partner in a Buffalo, New York law firm. He received a B.A. from Trinity College, a J.D. from the Washington University School of Law, and an LL.M. from the University of Pennsylvania School of Law. Mr. Friedman is the author of numerous legal articles and two prior books: *Sex Law: A Legal Sourcebook on Critical Sexual Issues for the Non-Lawyer* (McFarland & Co.); and *The Law of Parent-Child Relationships* (ABA Press). He concentrates his legal practice in the area of general business and corporate law.

Dedication

To our family business clients, past, present and future.

ACKNOWLEDGMENTS

We would like to acknowledge the support of our family who encouraged us to work through the occasional difficulties we encountered as a result of co-authoring this book several hundred miles apart from each other.

Thanks also to Nadine Lawicki (once again) and Valerie Licastro for their expert secretarial assistance in typing this manuscript.

Last, but not least, Scott would like to acknowledge the support of his wife, Lisa, and children, Samantha, Eliza, Julia and Madeline. Their continuing encouragement and understanding helped make this book possible.

PREFACE

A family business is one that is owned or controlled by one or more family members. Most businesses in the United States are family owned. They range from very small companies to well-known companies, such as Wal-Mart, Mars and Anheuser-Busch, that are worth many billions of dollars. Family businesses are created for a variety of reasons, but they generally share as a premise that family members can work together to accomplish their business objectives more profitably than if they worked alone. Notwithstanding the wide variety of family companies and the reasons why they were initially begun, there is, perhaps, also one common problem: most family businesses do not last through ownership by even the second generation. A family business that is owned by (or even principally owned by) the third or fourth generation is, indeed, rare. For many, the original premise of working together for shared goals is shattered by siblings and cousins who ruin the legacy that their parents and grandparents gave to them.

We believe that the American dream of building a business that can be passed on to your children, grandchildren and even great-grandchildren *can be realized!* We have written this book to help show you how.

After years of studying and representing many family businesses, we believe that success is directly correlated to understanding and planning. Those families that care to understand the issues they face and then plan strategies to address those issues have the best chance of prospering. Understanding does not, however, always come quickly or easily. Many families have "abdicated" their shared responsibility to their professional advisors — attorneys, accountants, financial advisors and the like — and have drifted so far away from critical issues that, in fact, these advisors know more about businesses than do their owners. Although many books have been written on business, most are too complicated for anyone but these same professionals to comprehend. More important, we are unaware of any book that has as its sole focus the legal issues facing family businesses. Our aim in writing this book is to provide easy-to-understand, practical information that can be put to immediate use by the readers and their families.

We have attempted to address the most important legal issues that typically face family businesses. Some of these issues are peculiar to family businesses and many are not. We wanted to write a book that the reader could use as a *single resource* on legal issues facing the family business without having to turn to multiple other resource guides. We have written this book as if the readers were our clients looking for useful and understandable general information. We assume, accordingly, an interested reader but one with no knowledge about this book's subject matter. The text is designed to be informative but easy to read. We believe that owners, family members and employees alike can better manage their business and related personal affairs by understanding the subjects discussed in this book. Time-tested strategies for success (which we refer to as "Strategic Tips") are liberally suggested throughout the book. We have, however, left for others the explanation of legal principles which do not raise issues "peculiar" to family businesses. Accordingly, subjects such as real estate, litigation, bankruptcy, taxation, and environmental law are not treated here. Finally, we have attempted to write a book for the purpose of explaining important legal principles to participants in family businesses—and not a book which offers psychological advice and counseling. There are already a number of useful books which fill this latter role. We hope that, with the aid of the suggestions we offer, the difficult emotional issues that are often raised in family businesses can be more satisfactorily resolved.

Because each family business is different, so will be the answers to each reader's questions and the solutions to each reader's problems. No book can substitute for a careful analysis of the specific facts and circumstances facing a family business by the family members themselves and their professional advisors. Our aim is to help make consultations with your advisors meaningful so you and your family remain "in the driver's seat" and continue to "call the shots." We are confident that you and your family can more profitably (and peacefully) enjoy the American dream of being part of a successful family business with a better understanding of the subjects discussed in this book.

INTRODUCTION

Family businesses share several common concerns. We believe that the four most important concerns for a typical family business are:

1. Operating Profitability

Every business (except for a charity) is run to make a profit. Family businesses are no different. If the business is losing money, it can be assumed that the owners will terminate the operation at some point. If a choice between two options exists, all else being equal, the family will choose the option that maximizes profits.

2. Controlling Important Business Decisions

Most entrepreneurs who start a business prefer to call the shots on major issues affecting their business. If there are two or more decision makers (such as father-son or brother-brother), the potential for dispute increases. Mechanisms designed to avoid disputes or facilitate resolution of disputes are good for business.

3. Business and Personal Assets Should Be Protected to the Greatest Extent Possible

Most business owners find it desirable to operate their business without jeopardizing their nonbusiness assets (such as home and savings). Accordingly, it is usually advantageous to set up and operate the business in a manner that does not expose the personal assets of the owner to liabilities incurred by the business. Similarly, where there are two or more family members who own a business, each owner presumably is concerned that the company's assets are protected from the personal debts of the other owner(s).

4. Ensuring That the Business Can Be Passed Down to Children and Future Generations

For a variety of reasons, many families prefer to keep ownership in the family's hands. Family objectives, values and personal agendas—both related and unrelated to direct company operations—are often best protected and enhanced by the family (and can be more easily challenged by nonfamily owners).

It is our experience that most business owners prefer to give their children the *option* of continuing the family business. Although owners may have widely differing feelings if their children choose *not* to pursue this option, we believe that most owners would be unhappy if this option, for one or more reasons, were to become unavailable.

☞ *STRATEGIC TIP*

We have written this book to show you how these four concerns can be addressed "up front" by proper planning and attention to various legal issues and options. We believe these four concerns are not always clearly spelled out nor clearly understood. Further, we believe that specific family and business plans are not always selected with these concerns in mind. On the contrary, we believe that many family businesses often make decisions on the basis of information that may be applicable to business generally—which, by pure chance, may produce good or bad results for the family business. Our aim is to help remove this element of chance so that whatever decision you reach, you will know why you are reaching it. In order to make this book as practical and helpful to you as possible, we have written it, first, to provide an understandable overview of various legal issues and, second, to suggest certain "strategic tips," which are intended to provoke your thinking on how such legal issues can be addressed in a manner which will serve you, not obstruct you.

Chapter One

Selecting Your Family Business Structure

F amily businesses are ordinarily conducted as (1) a sole proprietorship, (2) a general partnership, (3) a limited partnership, or (4) a corporation. In order to provide you with an understanding as to which of these forms is preferable for your family business, this chapter provides an overview of each of these four business forms and then considers how they differ with respect to (a) liability for business obligations; (b) decision-making responsibility (management); (c) tax treatment; and (d) ability to transfer ownership in the business to family and nonfamily members (transferability). Because the management and transfer of ownership of a family business are so important in making your analysis, yet also so complex, we devote separate chapters to these subjects. Our aim in this chapter is to give you a broad, but meaningful, overview of these alternative business forms. Consultations with your attorney and accountant may be especially useful to help you with this analysis.

Most lawyers and business advisors agree that there is no "best" form in which to run a business because the concerns and requirements for each business are unique. Some of these concerns may not be discussed here, yet may have extraordinary importance for your business. Also, we note that these various forms for operating a business can be organized and operated to emphasize certain elements more than others — such as control or limitations on liability — so that the forms may become more or less similar to each other in certain respects. This is an area where meaningful consultations with your attorney can be particularly useful. Nevertheless, with an understanding of the following factors, you should have a much better idea of which form is best suited for *your* business.

SOLE PROPRIETORSHIP

General Overview

A sole proprietorship simply refers to a business owned by an individual. A sole proprietorship is not a distinct legal entity existing separately from the individual. No formal steps are required to create or maintain a sole proprietorship. Accordingly, it is the simplest and cheapest way to set up and begin a business. A proprietor can operate the business under his name or under a fictitious name if a certificate (a "doing business as . . ." certificate) is filed with the appropriate state official. A proprietor can generally operate his business under any name he pleases so long as the name selected is not deceptive or confusingly similar to the name of an established business.

Liability of the Proprietor for Business Obligations

Because a sole proprietorship is not a "distinct legal entity" and thus does not exist separate and apart from its owner, a proprietor of a family business is personally liable for all of the debts and obligations of the business. This liability exposes all of the personal (not just the business) assets of the proprietor to liabilities incurred in the operation of the business. This liability includes (1) obligations incurred in the ordinary course of the business (such as lease rentals, purchase commitments and taxes) and (2) unanticipated obligations (such as claims arising from accidents caused by the business or failure of the business to comply with applicable laws and ordinances). Accordingly, a proprietor can lose more money than he originally invested in the business.

An example may be helpful. In 1993, John Smith opens a bookstore as a sole proprietorship under the fictitious (or trade) name "Owl Books." Smith signs a five-year lease of retail space and, together with a part-time employee, begins to sell books from this space. If Smith terminates the lease prior to its scheduled expiration date in 1998 (because, for example, he cannot afford this space or because sales are so good that he needs more space), he may be personally liable to the landlord for the balance of the unpaid rent. If Owl Book's assets are insufficient to cover the landlord's damages resulting from the lease termination, the landlord can seek to satisfy his claim from Smith's personal assets, including his house and savings account. In short, all of the assets of the proprietor, whether or not such assets have been used in conducting the business, are subject to claims of the proprietor's creditors if the business assets are insufficient to satisfy business debts.

☞ *STRATEGIC TIP*

Many family businesses are conducted as sole proprietorships because, among other reasons, the owners believe that their businesses are not fraught with risks or that unanticipated or unusually large liability claims may be handled through appropriate insurance coverage. Because not all business obligations can be covered (limited) by insurance, a family will want to exercise great caution in operating a business as a sole proprietorship.

Management of the Proprietorship

Management questions rarely arise when an individual engages in business as a sole proprietor because a sole proprietor has the right to manage the business as he sees fit. This right is based on the principle that each individual who has reached the age of majority and is mentally competent is ordinarily free to transact business without prior third-party approval or consent. Stated otherwise, in a sole proprietorship, there is no distinction between the owner and the manager of the business. Accordingly, in operating Owl Books, Mr. Smith can decide to sell only comic books and to open Owl Books only on Sunday evenings. A proprietor is free to hire one or more employees and/or managers who can be given broad decision-making powers, but such managers will be accountable to the proprietor. In order to provide a manager with incentives to do his job efficiently and conscientiously, a proprietor may give or sell him an ownership interest in the business (that is, a right to participate in the profits of the business). This by itself may convert the business from a sole proprietorship to a partnership.

☞ *STRATEGIC TIP*

A proprietor may, of course, enter into an employment agreement with an employee granting to the employee a right to a specified percentage of the profits of the business. Such a bonus arrangement does not necessarily mean that the employee is a partial owner of, or "partner" in, the business. He simply has a contractual right to receive a bonus. This arrangement may provide employees of a sole proprietorship with powerful financial incentives without requiring the proprietor to dilute his ownership interest in the business.

Tax Treatment

A sole proprietor's income and expense must be reported by the proprietor on his personal income tax return. The sole proprietor, although not subject to social security tax (because he does not receive wages), is generally subject to self-employment tax, which can result in paying taxes at a higher rate than if he were taxed as an employee!

A sole proprietor may feel the effect of the tax laws in a variety of ways. For example, assets that are acquired or converted for use in the business can generally be depreciated or amortized (i.e., "written off" over time as a business expense). Accordingly, you will want to consider with your professional advisors the impact of the tax laws.

Transferability of the Proprietorship

Sole proprietorships cannot be transferred to other individuals or businesses. However, the assets (and liabilities) comprising the business can be transferred by sale, gift or, at death, by will. When a proprietor dies, the assets of the business are included as assets of his estate. If the sole proprietor brings in another "owner" (as contrasted with an employee) to help him run the business and thereby share in the profits and losses, the proprietor may have (intentionally or not) transferred assets of his proprietorship to a partnership of which he is but one partner. Accordingly, careful attention should be given to planning and implementing such decisions.

☞ STRATEGIC TIP

For tax purposes, the sale of a proprietorship is treated as a sale of assets on an item-by-item basis. Depending on the tax basis of each asset, the sale could produce a tax gain or loss. A corporation (and all of its assets), by contrast, can be simply transferred by a sale of stock. Accordingly, selling a corporation may be less complicated from a tax-reporting perspective than selling a proprietorship.

GENERAL PARTNERSHIP

General Overview

A general partnership is a voluntary association of two or more individuals, corporations or other legal entities who agree to work together, sharing to some degree their profits (or losses) and control, for a common business purpose. Much like a sole proprietorship, only with two or more proprietors, no formal steps are *required* to create or maintain a general partnership. No formal meetings need be held; documents need not be prepared and signed; and filing or other fees ordinarily need not be paid. Most partners in a general partnership are actively involved in the operation of the business, although the term "silent partner" correctly suggests that some partners need not be active in partnership affairs. If John Smith and his sister, Amy, simply open Owl Bookstore together and begin operations, they have, in effect, created a partnership. The law does not uniformly recognize a general partnership as an entity separate and apart from its general partners. At times, under the so-called "entity theory," the law treats a general partnership as a separate legal entity. At other times, under the so-called "aggregation theory," the law treats a general partnership, not as a separate legal entity, but as simply the sum of its individual members.

☞ STRATEGIC TIP

Although a partnership can be formed without a written agreement between the partners, it may, as discussed in chapter two, be *desirable* for the partners to prepare and sign a written agreement to set forth their understanding on partnership affairs (i.e., management of the partnership activities, distribution of profits, allocation of losses, procedures for withdrawal of a partner from the partnership or for dissolution of the partnership, etc.). Such an agreement, which is essentially a "private contract," can often help the partners avoid or resolve their disputes with less hostility and more effectiveness.

☞ *STRATEGIC TIP*

There may be advantages and disadvantages to taking on a partner to help operate your business. Advantages typically include: (1) sharing workloads; (2) sharing expenses and financial risks; (3) utilizing special talents and resources; and (4) promoting an entrepreneurial and proprietary spirit in a valued worker. Disadvantages typically include: (1) having to share financial success; (2) relinquishing some management control; (3) having to work with people that you may come to dislike; and (4) exposing yourself to personal liability for actions taken by your partner in the course of the partnership's business, even if such actions were unknown to you or were inconsistent with an agreement between you and your partner. We suggest that you weigh these and other factors carefully *before* deciding to take on a partner.

Liability of Partners for Business Obligations

In a general partnership, each partner is personally liable for all of the debts and other obligations of the partnership. If the partnership assets are not sufficient to meet partnership obligations, the individual partners may be forced to satisfy such obligations out of their personal assets (i.e., non-partnership assets). A partner who pays a disproportionate percentage of a liability of the partnership may be able to seek contribution or reimbursement from a partner who has paid less than his proportionate share of the liability. In addition, a partner may seek reimbursement from another partner for incurring obligations to creditors that were not authorized by the partnership. The "culpable" partner, however, may not have sufficient (or even any) assets to reimburse his partners! Although operating a business as a general partnership exposes its general partners to personal liability, many family businesses — especially ones where family members trust each other — are conducted as general partnerships because of the minimal legal, accounting and similar steps that must be taken to create and maintain a general partnership.

☞ *STRATEGIC TIP*

Because of the financial exposure associated with being a general partner, persons contemplating the formation of, or entry into, a general partnership should satisfy themselves as to the financial condition of the partnership. Perhaps more important, because any single general partner may bind the partnership (and, in effect, the other partners) to contracts and other obligations, individuals should have a high level of trust and confidence in each other before becoming partners. This trust is recognized in law by the imposition of a "fiduciary obligation" on each partner—an obligation that each partner treats all other partners fairly. Although you may trust family members as prospective partners, you may also be aware of their personal foibles (gambling, for example) that may cause you to rethink the merits of proceeding with a partnership.

☞ *STRATEGIC TIP*

It may be possible for a general partnership to persuade certain of its creditors to look only to the business assets of the partnership and not to the personal assets of the individual partners to satisfy partnership obligations. An effort to limit the recourse of creditors by negotiation will generally only be available if the partnership can demonstrate to the creditors that the financial condition of the partnership is so healthy that access to the personal assets of the individual partners is unnecessary. However, in response to such arguments, creditors may simply say, "If the business is so good, why be concerned to limit your personal liability?" In any event, there may be particular family assets that you may nevertheless be able to protect as a result of such negotiation.

Management of the Partnership

In a general partnership, each general partner is an agent of the partnership and, in the absence of an agreement to the contrary, has an equal say in the management of the partnership. Because the general public that transacts business with the partnership cannot realistically be required to determine whether an agreement modifying this general principle of "equal authority" exists, the law provides that each partner has the authority to bind the partnership to contracts and other business arrangements. Accordingly, if a general partner signs a contract on behalf of the partnership with a third party in violation of the partnership agreement, the partner's signature, under the legal doctrine of "apparent authority," will be sufficient to bind the partnership.

☞ *STRATEGIC TIP*

An important exception to the doctrine of apparent authority provides that the partnership is not liable to a third party for a partner's action if the third party knew that the partner's actions violated the partnership agreement. As a result, sophisticated parties who transact business with partnerships customarily review applicable partnership documents as a matter of prudence to verify the existence (or absence) of any restrictions on the authority of a general partner. Because you cannot assume, however, that all parties who may deal with your partners will investigate such partners' authority, it remains important that you trust your partners.

Tax Treatment

The income and expenses of the partnership generally flow through directly to the partners, who report their share of income and expense on their personal tax returns. The partnership itself only files an "information return." Partners, like sole proprietorships, are not considered employees and may have to pay a self-employment tax. Partners also pay the same amount of tax regardless of whether the partnership income is characterized as salary, interest or profit.

☞ *STRATEGIC TIP*

Because there is no double level of taxation of partnership income (that is, income is not taxed first at the partnership level and then taxed at the individual partner level), operating a business as a partnership may be attractive from a tax perspective. In addition, partnerships generally provide the partners with greater flexibility than a corporation as to allocating income and losses among the partners. Historically, many family businesses were operated as partnerships in order to help "shift" income to minor children partners—whose income was lower than the income of their parents and hence taxed at a lower rate. Under the guidelines set forth by the U.S. Supreme Court in a case called *Culbertson vs. U.S.*, this technique to reduce taxes may be of questionable validity. In that case, the court held that a "partner" will not be recognized as a partner for *tax purposes* if he does not contribute something of value to the partnership. Accordingly, a minor child who is essentially inactive in a family partnership may not be considered a partner and, instead, his "income" will be attributed to his parents.

Transferability of General Partnership Interests

As a rule, a partner cannot transfer his interest in a partnership to another person without the consent of each of his other partners. Moreover, in the absence of an agreement to the contrary, dissolution of a partnership occurs whenever an existing partner ceases to be a partner, whether as a result of retirement, death, expulsion or the like. Furthermore, the bankruptcy of any partner may cause a dissolution of the partnership.

☞ *STRATEGIC TIP*

Partners of many larger partnerships agree that their partnerships are to continue in the event of a single partner's retirement, death, expulsion, bankruptcy, etc. in order to avoid the termination that would otherwise result when a partner ceases to be a partner. The relationship of the partners is simply reconstituted to give effect to the departure of a partner (or, conversely, the admission of a new partner). Provision should be made, of course, for disbanding the partnership when it is appropriate. By contrast, it is unusual for partnerships to stipulate ahead of time to admit individuals into the partnership in particular circumstances because the partners typically do not want unknown persons to be forced upon them as partners.

☞ *STRATEGIC TIP*

The laws governing the rights and obligations of partners and partnerships vary from state to state. Many states have adopted a uniform partnership statute, but with modification. Before forming or entering into a general partnership, you should consult with an attorney to assist you in evaluating whether the partnership laws in the state where the partnership will be formed or where it exists contain any unusual provisions.

LIMITED PARTNERSHIP

General Overview

A limited partnership is a distinct legal entity created under state statutory law. Unlike a general partnership, which can be formed by the oral agreement of two or more partners, a limited partnership is a creature of statute and is formed by complying with the filing requirements of the applicable state statute. Every limited partnership must have at least one general partner and one limited partner. The general and limited partners need not be individuals; they may be corporations, trusts or even other limited partnerships. In exchange for having only limited personal liability for partnership obligations, limited partners have very limited managerial authority in the partnership's activities.

☞ *STRATEGIC TIP*

A limited partnership may make sense if some family members seek only to invest in the business and have one or more other family members actively managing operations. The limited partnership form of business may not, however, be suitable if family members are active in the business and wish to participate in management decisions. If, for example, John Smith wants his wealthy sister, Amy, to invest in Owl Bookstore, which she is happy to do so long as she can remain inactive and is not liable for more than the amount of her investment, the limited partnership form may be suitable.

Liability of General and Limited Partners

As indicated above, all limited partnerships have at least one general partner and one limited partner. Absent fraud or other unusual circumstances, limited partners are liable for partnership obligations only to the extent of their investment in the partnership. The general partner(s) of a limited partnership, however, have unlimited personal liability for general partnership obligations. Put another way, if a creditor's claim or judgment against the partnership exceeds the assets of the partnership, the general partner's personal assets may be used to satisfy the claim or judgment. In short, the liability of a general partner of a limited partnership is no different than the liability of the general partner of a general partnership.

☞ *STRATEGIC TIP*

In order to protect himself against the unlimited personal liability faced by a general partner, a person contemplating serving as a general partner of a limited partnership may form a corporation, which, in turn, will serve as the general partner. Through his stock ownership of the corporate general partner, the person will effectively achieve the same control over the partnership's activities as if he were serving individually as the general partner. If more than one person is to serve as a general partner, each can either form his own corporation to serve as the general partner or such persons can split the stock of a single corporation, which will serve as the sole general partner.

Management of the Limited Partnership

A limited partnership is managed and controlled by its general partner(s). Limited partners have a voice in only a few areas pertaining to management of the partnership and, if they become excessively involved in partnership activities, they risk being treated as a general partner and facing unlimited liability for partnership obligations to third parties. This lack of control may not be particularly objectionable for limited partners who, while prepared to invest in a good idea, recognize their own inexperience in operating the partnership's business.

Tax Treatment

The tax treatment of limited partnerships, like the tax treatment of individuals, general partnerships and corporations, is extremely complex. Generally, if appropriate steps are taken in forming and operating the limited partnership, the double-level of taxation applicable to corporations (discussed below) will be inapplicable and the income and losses of the limited partnership will flow through the partnership directly to the individual partners in accordance with their interests in the partnership. Because of the flow-through nature of partnership losses, many wealthy individuals may be interested in investing in a limited partnership that, at least in the early years, will generate losses that can be used to reduce their other taxable income. However, restrictions on the use of passive losses may substantially reduce the benefit to such individuals of losses from their passive investments.

Transferability of Limited Partnership Interests

Partnership interests are not always freely transferrable. The transferability of general and limited partnership interests in a limited partnership is generally governed by provisions in the partnership agreement. As a matter of law, a general partner may usually withdraw from a limited partnership simply by notifying the other partners, but he will be liable to the other partners if the withdrawal violates the partnership agreement. Generally, a new general partner may be admitted to the partnership only with the consent of a specified percentage of the limited partners. The ability of a limited partner to withdraw from a limited partnership is also usually restricted by the partnership agreement.

☞ *STRATEGIC TIP*

Some state partnership statutes provide that a limited partner may not withdraw from the limited partnership prior to the dissolution of the partnership. Some statutes also provide that a limited partner may assign his limited partnership interest, but the consent of the general partner may be required as a condition to the effectiveness of such assignment. The assignee of such interest does not thereby obtain the rights of a partner, but only the right to receive the distributions (or right to use partnership losses on a tax return) which would otherwise have been paid to the assignor (i.e., the limited partner making the assignment). Accordingly, you will want to discuss the issue of transferability and assignability with your attorney so you know what is (and is not) permissible in your state.

CORPORATION

General Overview

Like a limited partnership, a corporation is recognized and treated as a distinct entity when properly created under state law. Whereas a limited partnership is owned by both its general and limited partners and managed solely by its general partners, a corporation is owned by its shareholders, managed by its directors, and run on a day-to-day basis by officers and other employees. The roles of each of these players on the corporate team are considered in chapter two. Because a corporation is a distinct legal entity, it (like a limited partnership) conducts business in its own name and not in the names of its shareholders. Each state requires that certain formal steps (e.g., the filing of articles of incorporation with appropriate state officials) be taken to create and maintain the existence of a corporation.

Liability of the Corporation and Shareholders for Business Obligations

Like a proprietorship or partnership, a corporation has unlimited liability for its business obligations. However, as a general rule, a corporation's *shareholders* (like the limited partners in a limited partnership) have no personal liability for the corporation's debts or other obligations beyond the value of their investments in the corporation. Accordingly, a family business conducted in corporate form helps protect the personal assets of the shareholder-owners from the liabilities incurred in the operation of the business. This "limited liability" is perhaps the single greatest advantage of conducting business in the corporate form. For example, an enormous damage award was imposed on Exxon several years ago as a result of the Alaskan oil spill. Although the shareholders of Exxon witnessed a reduction in the value of their shares of Exxon stock as a result of the award, they did not, simply by virtue of their ownership of Exxon, face personal responsibility for the damage award. Similarly, when Pennzoil sued Texaco for tortiously interfering with Pennzoil's contract with Getty, shareholders of Texaco witnessed a reduction in the value of their Texaco stock, but were not otherwise vulnerable to the claims of Pennzoil.

If John Smith had operated Owl Bookstore as a corporation, rather than as a sole proprietorship, Owl could probably have terminated its five-year lease early without exposing Smith's personal assets to a claim of the landlord. Of course, the landlord would have been able to recover damages out of any of the assets of Owl (such as its inventory, cash, accounts receivable and the like).

Corporate Formalities. In order to ensure their "limited liability," the shareholders of a corporation must operate their corporation with attention to particular rules and procedures — corporate formalities. Many small businesses find these formalities unduly burdensome and/or expensive. If, however, these corporate formalities are not complied with, shareholders risk exposing all of their personal assets to the corporation's creditors (having the corporation's veil of protection "pierced") if the assets of the business are insufficient to pay the claims of creditors in full. Some of these formalities are noted in chapter two, but you will want to discuss them with your attorney so that there is no question about your corporation's compliance with applicable requirements.

One commonly overlooked corporate formality involves the proper execution (signing) of documents by the corporation (and *not* by individual representatives of the corporation).

A shareholder, in his capacity as a shareholder, generally does not sign documents on behalf of his corporation. Ordinarily, the corporation acts through its officers. An officer of the corporation, such as the president or vice president, entering into a contract on behalf of his corporation should make sure that (1) the corporation's name appears on the signature page of the contract, (2) he signs his name below the name of the corporation, and (3) he specifies that he is signing in his capacity as an officer of the corporation. Failure by an officer to comply with the foregoing formalities may expose him to *personal* liability under the contract.

Illustrated below is the correct way to sign a contract on behalf of Owl Bookstore Corporation.

Owl Bookstore Corporation

By: _____
Name: *John Smith*
Title: *Vice President*

In the above illustration, Owl Bookstore Corporation is executing the contract and Smith, in his capacity as vice president of Owl, is simply signing for Owl.

Illustrated below is one common — yet *incorrect* way — to sign an agreement which is intended to be signed on behalf of Owl Bookstore Corporation:

By: _____
Name: *John Smith*
Title: *Vice President*

In the second illustration, a court might hold Mr. Smith personally liable under the agreement because he has not properly indicated that he is signing the agreement on behalf of Owl Bookstore Corporation, even though he has indicated that he is a vice president.

Adequate Capital. Courts have also "pierced the corporate veil" and held shareholders personally liable for obligations of the corporation if the corporation has not been adequately capitalized (i.e., "financed"). Whether or not a business has been adequately capitalized will depend upon the type of business being conducted. For example, a family-run taxi business which operates as a corporation may require substantially more capital than a bookstore to be considered reasonably capitalized. If Acme Taxi Corporation does not have assets in an amount which can reasonably be expected to defray the costs of operating a taxi business (including the cost of traffic accidents), a court may permit a pedestrian or passenger injured in a traffic accident caused by Acme Taxi to sue both the corporation and its shareholders for personal injury. Accordingly, the shareholders must determine with their professional advisors the minimum level of capital that should be maintained by the corporation, in light of the business activities of the corporation and the types of insurance it maintains, to prevent the corporate veil from being pierced.

Personal Guarantees. Because a corporation generally confers limited liability on the shareholders, parties entering into an agreement with a relatively unknown corporation or one with limited assets will commonly insist that the shareholders personally guarantee the corporation's obligations. Although giving a personal guarantee may eliminate a primary benefit of operating in the corporate form, a shareholder will not be personally liable for corporate obligations which he has not personally guaranteed. Accordingly, it may be possible for a shareholder to intelligently select those corporate obligations which he is prepared to personally "backup." Finally, it is possible that the shareholder of a corporation may, apart from the corporation, be *personally* liable for injuries caused by his own negligence. For example, the owner/driver of a taxi that hits a pedestrian may be liable in his capacity as a driver. Insurance can help both a corporation and its shareholders "manage" the problem of such potential liability.

☞ *STRATEGIC TIP*

A federal court of appeals recently found that the sole shareholder of a real estate company could be held personally liable for his employees' racially discriminatory sales practices — even if he was not aware of such practices. The court based its conclusion on the finding that a sole shareholder has the power to control his employees' actions. While it is too early to predict whether this decision will be followed by other courts, controlling shareholders should consider instituting appropriate corporate policies to help eliminate illegal forms of discrimination.

Management of the Corporation

A corporation is owned by its shareholders. Shareholders may be "divided" into more than one "class," depending on the attributes of the stock they own. For example, some shareholder classes may have voting rights and other may have no (or only limited) voting rights. The shareholders having voting rights elect the board of directors, typically at the annual meeting of shareholders. The board of directors in turn controls the overall management and direction of the corporation. The board generally delegates day-to-day operating authority of the corporation to corporate officers (e.g., president, vice president, secretary, treasurer). Although certain major corporate decisions require shareholder authorization (such as a determination to increase the authorized capital of the corporation, to dissolve the corporation, to sell all or substantially all of the assets of the corporation, or to merge the corporation into another corporation), most actions by a corporation (such as entering into routine contracts, borrowing money, establishing the level of executive compensation and declaring dividends) may be authorized solely by the board of directors.

☞ *STRATEGIC TIP*

In family-controlled businesses, the shareholders typically elect themselves (or loyal and responsive individuals) as directors. In such cases, an identity is shared by the shareholders and directors. As the number of shareholders of a corporation increases, the distinction between *ownership* and *management* of the corporation becomes more pronounced. Occasionally, differences develop between the views of shareholders (the owners) and those of the board of directors. These differences frequently cause family businesses to falter and fail. How these differences are resolved is an important aspect of corporate law and is discussed in chapter two.

Tax Treatment

Unlike proprietorships and partnerships, a corporation (referred to as a "C corporation" under federal tax law) is considered by the

IRS to be a separate taxable entity. As a result, a corporation pays tax on the net income it earns. Its shareholders also include in their income amounts distributed to them by the corporation as dividends. This results in the so-called "double level of taxation." Some corporations are able to avoid the double level of taxation to which C corporations and their shareholders are generally subject. A corporation with no more than thirty-five shareholders, each of whom is a U.S. citizen, resident alien, an estate or a qualifying trust, may elect "S corporation" status under federal (and sometimes state) law. Detailed rules have been developed by the IRS to determine who should be counted for purposes of measuring the thirty-five shareholder limitation. In general, an S corporation is not subject to a corporate-level income tax; rather, the corporation's income and expenses are passed through directly to the shareholders who then report their pro rata share of the income and expenses on their personal tax returns. Unlike a C corporation, an S corporation may have only one class of stock. Accordingly, if shareholders wish to allocate corporate control and economic returns in a different fashion for different shareholders, an S corporation may not be suitable. For example, if one shareholder wants to acquire an investment that bears a mandatory annual dividend and other shareholders are content to accept the returns offered or projected for common stock only, accommodation of the differing objectives may require either use of a C corporation or a limited partnership. The tax aspects of corporations are particularly complicated and you will want to discuss such aspects carefully with your advisors.

☞ STRATEGIC TIP

In order to avoid the double tax applicable to C corporations, smaller corporations commonly seek to distribute all of their excess earnings (i.e., earnings which need not be retained for the corporation's future growth or operations) to shareholders in the form of increased salaries. Although each shareholder-employee must include the increased salary in his taxable income, a corporation is permitted to deduct such salary payments as a business expense in calculating its net taxable income. If, however, a corporation pays its shareholders salaries that are materially higher than the general norm for similarly situated employees in other businesses (who are not also owners), the Internal Revenue Service may "recharacterize" a portion of the "salary" payments as nondeductible dividends. Such IRS recharacterizations may be accompanied by monetary penalties.

Transferability of Corporate Interests

The law confers upon corporations an "unlimited life," which is terminable only upon shareholder vote or, in unusual cases, court or government order. Unlike interests in partnerships, shares of a corporation are, as a general rule and subject to applicable federal and state securities laws, freely transferable. However, the owners of many family businesses impose contractual restrictions on the transferability of shares to ensure that ownership of the business remains within the family. These contractual restrictions may take a variety of forms (such as flat prohibitions on transfer, a right of first refusal or a right of first offer) and are discussed extensively in chapter four.

SELECTING THE STRUCTURE OF YOUR FAMILY BUSINESS

Although each business must evaluate the approach best suited to achieving its unique objectives, we offer the following guidelines to help you select the structure for your family business:

Discount All Forms That Are Unavailable

Your first step in selecting a form of business should be to discount those forms which are legally or practically unavailable. For example, if two or more family members are interested in going into business, a sole proprietorship is, by definition, unavailable. We emphasize, however, that a general partnership is essentially a proprietorship with more than one owner. Accordingly, if a proprietorship is preferable to a corporation, the partnership will also likely be preferable to a corporation. Also, for example, if a business has more than thirty-five family members or outside investors or if it wishes to create more than one class of stock, it will not be eligible for S corporation status.

Review Your Business Objectives Against Each Business Form's Structural Capability to Meet Those Objectives

This chapter is designed to highlight certain important differences among the respective business forms in regard to four issues that are typically important to every business: (1) liability, (2) management, (3) tax treatment, and (4) transferability of ownership interests. Selecting the best form for your family business involves the careful exercise of judgment because the importance of these concerns are different for every business. Because no two businesses are alike, the merits of one form or another are different as well. We suggest that an intelligent decision as to which form is right for you should include consideration of these factors:

Liability. Some business forms are safer than others. If you believe your business is relatively safe, consider operating as a proprietorship, general partnership, or general partner in a limited partnership. If you are more concerned about risky aspects of your business operations, consider operating as a corporation.

☞ STRATEGIC TIP

Determine the importance of limiting your liability. Often, especially in start-up businesses, insurance can address many of your liability concerns. In "risky" businesses (where the likelihood of causing personal injuries is higher), limiting liability may be more important.

Management. Determine who will have an ownership interest in your business and then determine how it will be managed. If each owner insists on some management position, a limited partnership form will be inappropriate. A corporation may offer shareholders an added measure of "managerial influence" but, perhaps, not much more than that offered to limited partners. Accordingly, identify who the owners of your business will be and then determine how much of a day-to-day say in business operations they will require. This analysis will help focus your decision on suitable business forms.

☞ STRATEGIC TIP

In family businesses, the owners are often the managers. Both partnerships and corporations can be structured to accommodate a virtually unlimited form of management structure. Nevertheless, corporations may offer planning advantages because of the distinct roles assigned to owners (shareholders) and managers (directors and officers). As the size of a business increases — and the number of family members involved in the business increases as well – the corporate form may be preferable.

Tax Treatment. Determine the various tax consequences (savings or liabilities) your business would face if it were operated as a proprietorship, partnership or corporation. Then compare these consequences to determine which business form is cheapest and which is most expensive.

☞ *STRATEGIC TIP*

Tax planning can be one of the most important aspects in helping to ensure that your business operates profitably. You should discuss with your attorney and accountant how the ever-changing tax laws may affect the selection of your business form. We recommend that, among other subjects, you discuss:

1. **Personal vs. Corporate Tax Rates.** Prior to enactment of the Revenue Reconciliation Act of 1993, the maximum personal tax rate was 31 percent (vs. 34 percent for corporations), thus making it generally preferable to be taxed personally, and so to do business as a proprietorship, partnership or S corporation. The tax rates have changed under the 1993 Act, with a new effective maximum tax rate for individuals of 39.6 percent and a new maximum rate of 35 percent for coporations. As a result of these changes, your selection of the most desirable form of business, from a tax perspective, should be carefully considered to determine its real impact on your family business.

2. **Double vs. Single Taxation.** A regular corporation (or C corporation) is taxed as a separate entity, so its earnings are taxed and then its distributed earnings (dividends) are taxed to its shareholders. An S corporation avoids this double tax. Because of the double tax on C corporations, there are few instances in which you would select C corporation status over S corporation status, all other things being equal. If the business plans future acquisitions, C corporation status may be desirable because of the requirement that S corporations may not own subsidiary corporations.

3. **Employee Benefit Plans.** Before 1982, C corporations were often selected because of their eligibility to use employee benefit plans unavailable to other business forms. In that year, however, the Tax Equity and Fiscal Responsibility Act eliminated many restrictions so that, with minor exceptions, employee benefit plan-

ning is a neutral factor in the selection of business form. C and S corporations may both, however, offer certain employee benefit opportunities, such as Employee Stock Ownership Plans (ESOPS), Incentive Stock Option Plans, etc., which are unavailable to partnerships and proprietorships. You may wish to consider the types of employee benefit plans available under the different forms of business.

4. Offsetting Your Income Against Business Losses. Many new businesses lose money in their early years of operation. It may be advantageous for the individual investors to use these business losses on their personal returns. This can be accomplished through a partnership, proprietorship, or S corporation, but not a C corporation. If the business later begins making profits, it can be incorporated at a later date.

5. Compare Tax Basis Rules. A partnership's obligations to non-partners become part of each partner's tax basis in accordance with his pro rata share of the partnership. In an S corporation, however, a shareholder's tax basis is limited to the sum of his contributions to capital, his share of profits allocated to him, and loans by the shareholder to the corporation. Thus, the tax basis may be greater in a partnership than in an S corporation, which may afford a partner a greater opportunity to deduct business losses.

Transferability of Ownership Interests. Transferability issues can be considered in two respects: (1) transferring ownership of your business to unrelated parties as part of the sale or liquidation of the business, and (2) transferring ownership of your business to your family (spouse, children, etc.) as part of your estate plan and desire to continue as a family business. A consideration of estate planning opportunities can be especially useful when determining your business structure.

☞ *STRATEGIC TIP*
_____

Review with your advisors how you can transfer ownership of your business to your children with a minimum of income, estate and gift tax. This subject is considered at length in chapter eight. Because corporations can conveniently "split" ownership interests by issuing shares of stock, this form may offer important estate-planning benefits because of the comparative ease of transferring a stock certificate as opposed to title to particular business assets.

Consider Your Willingness to Adhere to Corporate Formalities

Partnerships (especially general partnerships) are usually less expensive to form and maintain than are corporations. A partnership can also be operated with less formality than is required by corporations. You should consider whether you and your family are temperamentally suited to adhering to the sometimes strict formalities associated with the operation of a business in corporate form.

Opportunities to Raise Capital

Because one of the most important aspects of operating a family business involves raising sufficient capital to meet the requirements of the business, the entire third chapter of this book is devoted to this subject. For purposes of the present discussion on forms of business organizations, we simply note that a business can raise money by borrowing (debt) or by giving a new investor a piece of the business (equity). Although proprietors, partners and corporations can all conveniently borrow money, only corporations and limited partnerships can conveniently raise money by issuing equity. This factor may influence the selection of a business form.

Consider Changing Forms as Your Business Develops

Although this chapter suggests a variety of factors you should consider in selecting the form of your family business, we emphasize that there is no formula or litmus test which can be used to select the best form for any business. Your decision should consider a variety of tax and non-tax factors and should be made in cooperation with your attorney and accountant. It is important to recognize that your decision is not "fixed in stone" but can be reevaluated over the life of your business. Choices can often be improved upon. In fact, it may even make sense to assume that you *will* be changing business forms as your business develops. For example, you may (1) start your own business as a proprietorship (relying on your own time and money); then (2) expand your business into a partnership by taking on a partner (who can contribute more money and services); then (3) incorporate your business as an S corporation to secure limited liability and available tax benefits; and, finally (4) convert your S corporation into a C corporation in the event the number of shareholders increases to more than thirty-five.

In short, by considering a variety of factors and by remaining flexible to adapt your business to meet changing circumstances, you should be able to select the best form(s) of business for your needs.

Chapter Two

Forming and Managing Your Business

O nce you decide which form is right for your family business, you may then wish to (or need to) take certain steps to properly establish your business in this chosen form. Once established, the business must also be properly managed to help ensure its success: a "chain of command" should be established to ensure that the right people have responsibility for making the variety of decisions your business will face. This chapter first provides an overview of how to establish your business and then provides an overview of how to manage the business.

FORMING YOUR PROPRIETORSHIP

In most states, a business owner who operates his business as a sole proprietorship can simply begin business operations without the need to satisfy any particular legal requirements. Forming a proprietorship is clearly the easiest business form to begin operations. Consider carefully all state and local requirements for operating a business. For example, your locality may require you to secure a permit which authorizes you to engage in a particular type of business. Businesses that deal directly with the public—e.g., restaurants and contractors—typically must get licenses or permits from an appropriate governmental agency. A sole proprietorship which pays wages to employees must secure an employer identification number from the IRS. As the sole owner and manager, the proprietor is not required to hold regular meetings to formally report on the state of the proprietorship (unlike corporations).

☞ *STRATEGIC TIP*

Ordinarily, if you conduct business as a sole proprietorship under a fictitious or trade name, you must file a "DBA Certificate" (a "doing business as" certificate) with the secretary of state of your state and, perhaps, the local clerk of your municipality. Such certificate must usually be displayed prominently at your place of business in order that the public has notice of whom it is dealing with. If your business operates in other states, you may need to obtain similar licenses or certificates authorizing such activities in those states.

☞ *STRATEGIC TIP*

Although a sole proprietorship is technically not required to establish its own bank accounts, it is useful to do so in order that business expenses can be deducted and substantiated upon audit. Without such substantiation, business expenses may be recharacterized as nondeductible *personal* expenses.

MANAGING YOUR PROPRIETORSHIP

As the "sole owner" of his business, the sole proprietor has the exclusive right to manage the business as he sees fit. This management prerogative extends to all decisions, from day-to-day decisions to long-range policy issues. The sole proprietor has both the power and right to make all decisions affecting his business. As a practical matter, when a sole proprietorship becomes big enough, the proprietor may want or need to hire employees to handle certain responsibilities. These employees can be asked to fill virtually any role required by the business, from the most ministerial and mundane to the most challenging and important roles. Indeed, although relatively unusual with this business form, it is possible (by delegating sufficient authority) to establish a separation between ownership and management.

☞ *STRATEGIC TIP*

As your sole proprietorship grows in size and number of employees, you will want to revisit the question of the suitability of this form of business. As a sole proprietor, you will have full *personal* liability for the debts of the business *and* for the acts committed by your employees in the scope of their employment. As the business grows, it may become impossible to monitor all of your employees' actions. Because the financial risk associated with being personally responsible for such employees' actions usually becomes too great, many sole proprietorships incorporate to secure limited personal liability.

FORMING YOUR GENERAL PARTNERSHIP

As indicated in chapter one, a general partnership is a voluntary association of two or more individuals, corporations or other legal entities who work together for a common business purpose. No formal steps are required to form a general partnership. All that is required is (1) an intention by the partners to carry on a business as co-owners; and (2) an agreement, whether expressed or implied, to share the profits and control of the business. In fact, people may, by operation of law, unintentionally become partners. One partner may delegate most or all of the management issues to another partner (a so-called "silent partner") as long as the right to participate in control is reserved.

Filing Requirements

Many states require a general partnership to file a certificate indicating the name and address of each partner in the county in which it does business. Although this requirement does not affect the relationship of the partners between themselves, it may preclude the partnership from using the legal system (including bringing a lawsuit) if no filing is made.

Put Your Partnership Agreement in Writing

Although no formal steps are required to create or maintain a general partnership, we recommend that the partners enter into a written partnership agreement to help clarify the rights and responsibilities partners have and owe to each other. Such agreements also help minimize the likelihood of disputes arising among the partners. Without a written agreement, the law of the state in which your partnership is in business implies certain standard terms to deal with many common scenarios. These terms, however, may be wholly inadequate for the partners. A partnership agreement lets you tailor your understanding so as to reduce the likelihood of dispute among your partners. The basic areas that should be covered by a written partnership agreement are addressed in chapter four.

☞ *STRATEGIC TIP*

The head of a family partnership may desire to bring additional family members into the partnership for a variety of reasons, including facilitating succession of ownership by his children. A partnership agreement can be drafted to ensure that decision-making authority remains vested with the family leader even though his ownership interest is diluted by transfers to his children and/or other heirs. A partnership agreement can provide that such "control" can be transferred to the successors very quickly or very gradually, depending on the wishes of the family.

MANAGING YOUR PARTNERSHIP

The management of a partnership is more complex than the management of a sole proprietorship, yet typically simpler than the management of a corporation. There is no requirement that general partnerships hold annual meetings. Decisions are made at meetings which can be regularly scheduled or called from time to time as necessary. Although regular meetings may not be required by law, such meetings are typically desirable to help keep partners informed about the affairs of the partnership. This may be especially true if some family members are relatively inactive yet interested partners.

Ordinarily, all partners have an equal voice in the management of the partnership unless they agree otherwise. Most decisions require majority approval; some decisions, depending on partnership agreement or state law, may require two-thirds or unanimous approval. As their size increases, many partnerships find it desirable to provide one partner or a small group of partners with authority to manage partnership affairs and make certain decisions affecting the partnership without first having to secure approval by all of the partners.

Management and decision-making questions that may arise in operating a partnership may become complicated by the fact that a partner may have the *authority* to act although he may not have the *right* to act. For example, one partner in a two-person partnership may have the authority (by virtue of the doctrine of "apparent authority") to bind the partnership to an office lease for the next five years, yet not have the right to do so without having first secured his partner's approval. Disputes among partners often arise because one partner seeks to make a decision for the partnership without having first secured the actual authority or right to do so. A carefully prepared partnership agreement which defines what partners can and cannot do may help eliminate this potential problem.

Many partnerships find it useful to divide management issues into two categories: (1) issues affecting the very nature, purpose and constituency of the partnership; and (2) issues which affect the operation of the partnership. In the absence of an agreement to the contrary, the first type of issues must be decided by unanimous approval of the partnership, while the second type of issues are ordinarily decided by simple majority of the partners in the partnership. Accordingly, as we will see below, making management decisions which fundamentally affect the partnership may be more difficult to do than making such decisions in a corporation (where it is possible to make fundamental corporate changes without unanimous approval of the stockholders). You should consider this factor in determining the best form of business for you and your co-owners.

FORMING YOUR LIMITED PARTNERSHIP

A limited partnership, which must have one or more general partners and one or more limited partners, is formed upon the filing of a certificate of limited partnership with the secretary of state of the particular state in which the limited partnership is being formed. Generally, a limited partnership certificate must include the name of the partnership, the names and addresses of each general partner and the partnership's registered address. Many states do not require the identification of the limited partners in the certificate, which may offer a measure of privacy to an investor.

Ensure Tax Status

As indicated in chapter one, limited partnerships are often selected as a form of business in order to take advantage of the federal income tax treatment of partnerships. Simply describing an entity as a limited partnership and making the filing prescribed by state law, however, may not ensure that the "limited partnership" will be treated as such for federal income tax purposes. The IRS regulations provide that a limited partnership will be "recharacterized" and taxable as a corporation, if its "corporate" attributes outnumber its "noncorporate" attributes. These regulations generally provide that corporate attributes consist of (1) centralized management, (2) continuity of existence, (3) limited liability, and (4) free transferability of interests. In order to ensure that a limited partnership is taxed as a partnership, and not as a corporation, it must have no more than two of the four preceding characteristics. Therefore, it is important to make sure that a limited partnership is structured in such a way as to ensure that its "noncorporate" characteristics outnumber its "corporate" characteristics. For example, one way to avoid the corporate characteristic of "free transferability of interests" is to provide in the partnership agreement that the general partner must approve all transfers of partnership interests. Also, most limited partnerships have a fixed life, perhaps twenty years, to avoid the corporate characteristic of continuity of existence.

Put Your Limited Partnership Agreement in Writing

The reasons given earlier for putting a general partnership agreement in writing are equally applicable with regard to limited partnerships. In addition, because of the fact that limited partners have little, if any, managerial control, it is important to set forth in the limited partnership agreement restrictions on the rights of the general partner(s). Such "veto" rights may restrict the ability of the general partner to take certain actions without first obtaining the consent of a specified percentage of the limited partners. For example, a limited partnership agreement may prevent a general partner from selling certain assets of the business without the consent of a majority in number (and/or in percentage interest) of the limited partners.

☞ STRATEGIC TIP

Some thought should be given to whether your limited partnership agreement should make appropriate provisions for conversion of the business to a general partnership. Although the limited partnership form may make sense today, a limited partner's heirs may wish to take a more active managerial role in the family business than would be permitted of a limited partner.

MANAGING YOUR LIMITED PARTNERSHIP

Management responsibility of a limited partnership is vested in the general partner(s). Limited partners have little, if any, say in the operation of the limited partnership although, as indicated above, many have contractual veto rights to prevent the general partner from taking certain actions. The fact that general partners may generally control the operations of a limited partnership without seeking approval of limited partners does not mean the general partner is free to operate the business for his own benefit and to the detriment of the limited partners. To the contrary, a general partner owes a fiduciary duty to his limited partners and, as such, must act in a fair and reasonable manner and avoid actions designed to benefit himself at the expense of the limited partners.

FORMING YOUR CORPORATION

Preincorporation Matters

Prior to forming your corporation, you will want to consider the most appropriate state in which to incorporate. For most family businesses, it makes sense to incorporate the business in the state where the business is physically located and where most of the shareholders reside. For large businesses, the state selected as the state of incorporation may have greater significance because states vary in terms of the rights they afford shareholders as well as the level of taxation.

It may be advantageous to enter into a formal "preincorporation agreement" with (1) parties with whom the corporation will do business after incorporation, and (2) parties who will serve as incorporators, shareholders and directors. With respect to the first group, such an agreement may address the entering into of contracts with such parties and the corporation (including the consequences if the corporation is not formed or fails to perform the contract). With respect to the second group, such an agreement may provide who are to serve as directors, who are to serve as officers (and at what salaries), and what share transfer restrictions may apply. In many respects, such preincorporation agreements can be similar to shareholders' agreements, but, technically, the latter are typically considered relevant only *after* incorporation.

How to Incorporate Your Business

A corporation is formed by filing articles of incorporation with the secretary of state of the particular state in which the corporation is being formed. The information that is typically required to be included in the articles of incorporation includes: (1) the name of the corporation, (2) the registered office of the corporation, (3) the purpose of the corporation, (4) the term for which the corporation is to exist, and (5) the authorized capital of the corporation. The following discussion provides some insight into how you may want to complete your articles of incorporation. Although the process is simple and routine, a failure to comply with applicable requirements can result in the establishment of an unintended partnership—which, of course, does not offer the limited liability features of the corporation. Most state corporation laws have sought to address this problem by providing that a corporation will be deemed to have been duly incorporated if the articles of incorporation are accepted for filing by the secretary of state.

Selecting a Name. Once a decision has been made to form a corporation, a name must be selected. A corporate name need not bear any resemblance to the name of the owners of the corporation. However, a corporate name will not be accepted by the state office responsible for incorporations if the name is the same as, or confusingly similar to, the name of any other existing corporation in the same state or one that is doing business in the state. Most state corporation statutes permit a person to reserve a corporate name for a brief period of time (e.g., 120 days) for the benefit of a corporation that is planning to be formed in the near future.

If your request for a particular corporate name is rejected because another person has previously utilized the name, you may be able to convince such person to give (or sell) the rights in the name to you for use in your business. Like a sole proprietorship, a corporation is generally permitted by state law to select a fictitious name by making an appropriate filing with the applicable state official. We recommend that a name be selected which either helps identify your products, your business or the owners. This can help your customers remember your business.

Registered Office. The articles of incorporation must identify a registered office of the corporation in the state where the corporation is being formed so that service of legal process and delivery of tax and other government forms may be made relatively conveniently. This does not mean that a shareholder must actually reside in the state of incorporation because "service agents" are available to act as such office. For example, if a shareholder living in California wishes to form a Delaware corporation but does not have a place of business in Delaware, he can designate, at modest cost, a service company doing business in Delaware as the registered address of the corporation. The service company, in its capacity as agent of the corporation, will then forward to the shareholder(s) any official notices it receives regarding the corporation.

The "Purpose" of Your Corporation. The articles of incorporation must identify the purpose of the corporation. It is now customary simply to state in the articles of incorporation that the corporation is being formed "for any lawful purpose." By stating the purpose of the corporation this broadly, the incorporating shareholders avoid the need to amend the articles should the purpose of the corporation change at some future date.

☞ STRATEGIC TIP

It is usually desirable to provide that the purpose of a corporation is to engage in any lawful business, in order that the business can efficiently take advantage of attractive business opportunities, even if such opportunities are in new arenas. Shareholders with a minority ownership interest who are concerned about losing their voice in the affairs of a corporation may, however, seek to limit the purpose of a corporation and so make it more difficult (or impossible) for the controlling faction to pursue such "tangential" opportunities. Thus, a family member who invests in a corporation formed to sell books may be able to preclude that corporation from opening a "fast food" franchise operation without his consent.

The Term of Your Corporation. Most corporations are formed without a fixed term. That is, the corporation's existence will continue perpetually unless affirmative steps are taken (e.g., dissolution or merger) to terminate it. Family businesses operated in corporate form are, accordingly, able to be passed from generation to generation simply by the transfer of stock in the corporation.

The Capital Structure of Your Corporation. The capital structure of a corporation simply refers to the number of shares of stock, and the kind of stock, that a corporation is authorized to issue. As a general rule, authorized capital consists of common stock and, if desirable, preferred stock as well. The "attributes" of the stock can be varied to fit the needs of the business and the shareholders. For example, common stock may consist of voting common stock and/or nonvoting common stock. Preferred stock, which also can be varied, generally differs from common stock in respect to its holder's rights upon liquidation (i.e., termination of the corporation), dividends and voting. Whereas holders of common stock are entitled to receive dividends only when and if declared by the board of directors (who are under no obligation to declare a dividend), holders of preferred stock may have a contractual right to receive dividends at stated times and in fixed amounts. Similarly, upon liquidation of a corporation and discharge of all debts and liabilities, holders of preferred stock may have a "preferential" right to a liquidation distribution before holders of common stock are entitled to receive anything. In exchange for such preferences, preferred shareholders have more limited opportunities than do owners of common stock to enjoy in the growth or success of the corporation. Once a corporation has been formed and its authorized capital established, the board of directors will determine the price at which the stock is sold and the identity of the purchasers. A corporation's authorized capital may be changed by an amendment to the articles. Such an amendment will generally require the approval of shareholders.

A corporation's capital structure can be flexibly established or modified to help allocate ownership interests and managerial control in virtually any possible fashion. This flexibility is extremely useful in trying to accommodate the varying interests that participants in a business may have. For example, if a five-person family wants to lodge control of the business in two shareholders but provide that all five family members participate equally in the profits of the business, their objective may be accomplished by creating a class of voting and nonvoting common stock. The two "active" shareholders could each be given twenty shares of voting common stock, and the three "inactive" members could each be given twenty shares of nonvoting common stock. Similarly, "senior" family members may be more interested in receiving a steady cash flow, while "junior" family members may be more interested in sacrificing current cash flow in order to build their family business for the future. Such competing interests can sometimes be conveniently accommodated by issuing the senior family members preferred stock which pays annual dividends (but which has little growth potential), and issuing the junior family members common stock (which may have little or no annual dividends but which represents the ownership interest with the growth potential). Corporate lawyers may spend a great deal of their time helping owners of a corporation allocate their respective investments and interests in a corporation by revising the corporation's capital structure.

☞ *STRATEGIC TIP*

Keep in mind that an S corporation may not have two classes of stock, and hence the amount of flexibility afforded by the corporate form may be limited if maintaining "S" status is desirable.

Advertising Your Corporation's Formation. A corporation commences its existence upon the filing (and acceptance) of the certificate of incorporation. Most states require that a brief notice be published by the incorporators of a corporation in a local newspaper, indicating that the corporation has been formed. You will, of course, want to verify the particular requirements in your state.

Having Your Organizational Meeting

After the articles of incorporation have been filed with the secretary of state or other appropriate state official and the corporation has been formed, an "organizational meeting" must be held. The purpose of this meeting is to permit the incorporators (those person(s) who actually formed the corporation, such as an attorney, paralegal or secretary) to select the initial director(s) of the corporation. Once selected, the directors can take certain steps to organize the corporation, including: (1) adopting bylaws of the corporation; (2) selecting officers of the corporation; and (3) issuing share certificates to the owners to reflect their respective ownership interests in the corporation. For convenience, most states permit these matters to be done by "written consents," without the requirement of an actual meeting. In other words, the incorporator simply executes a resolution (sometimes referred to as a written consent in lieu of a meeting) designating the initial directors of the corporation. The directors then execute a similar resolution adopting the bylaws, selecting the officers and the like.

☞ *STRATEGIC TIP*

Although written consents can dispense with the requirement to hold meetings for shareholders and directors, we have found that such meetings can be a valuable opportunity for family members to provide information, exchange ideas, voice concerns, and, more generally, "feel involved." Accordingly, we recommend actually having such meetings if practical.

Bylaws. The bylaws of a corporation constitute a contract among shareholders of the corporation that governs the relationship among the shareholders. Although there is no requirement that the bylaws address any specific matters, bylaws typically address the following:

1. Shareholder Meetings. Bylaws specify the procedures for scheduling and holding regular and special shareholder meetings. Many bylaws specify: (a) the minimum notice that must be given to shareholders in advance of a meeting (typically ten days); and (b) the minimum number of shares that must be present (or represented by proxies) at a meeting in order to have a "quorum" such that a shareholder meeting can proceed (typically a majority). Bylaws may also specify procedures—such as voting, adjourning, etc.—for conducting the meeting.

☞ *STRATEGIC TIP*

If there are two or more families (or factions of one family) holding shares in a corporation, it may be useful to provide that a certain amount of shareholder representation from each family or faction be present at a meeting in order to constitute a quorum. This can help ensure that one such faction is not "frozen out" of the decision-making process merely because it was unable to attend a meeting.

2. Board of Directors. Bylaws may specify the number of directors of the corporation, the qualifications the directors are required to have (such as a minimum age), and the term of office. Although it is common for all directors of a corporation to be elected or reelected annually to the board, the bylaws of many corporations provide for "staggered" terms for directors. Where a board has directors serving staggered terms, only a portion of the board comes up for reelection in any given year. This is useful where shareholders contemplate the possibility of a transition in board membership but desire to ensure a degree of continuity in board membership from year to year. The responsibilities of directors are discussed later in this chapter.

☞ *STRATEGIC TIP*

Where two or more families have ownership interests in one corporation, it may be desirable to provide in the bylaws (or shareholders' agreement) that each family is entitled to select a certain number of directors. Such a provision may help ensure adequate representation of the respective family interests.

If two or more families have equal ownership interests in a corporation (and so equal number of directors), it may be desirable to create an additional directorship, filled by a neutral nonfamily member, who could cast a tie-breaking vote in the event the families are deadlocked on an issue. This solution, of course, requires the family owners to leave their business fate in the hands of an outsider. Obviously, each family must consider the usefulness of this solution to its own circumstances.

3. Officers. Bylaws may specify the officers of the corporation and delineate the responsibilities of the officers. Most corporations have a president, a secretary and a treasurer. In addition, many corporations have one or more vice presidents, assistant secretaries and assistant treasurers. The responsibilities of corporate officers are discussed later in this chapter.

☞ *STRATEGIC TIP*

Where two or more families have ownership interests in one corporation, it may be desirable to provide that each family be responsible for selecting one or more officer positions. For example, if one family member serves as president of the corporation, a member of the second family may serve as treasurer and secretary. This division of responsibility can provide a healthy system of checks and balances.

Bylaws commonly provide that in the event a director or officer is sued as a result of actions taken by him in his capacity as a director or officer of the corporation, the corporation will indemnify him and hold him harmless against any resulting judgments so long as the actions of the director or officer do not reflect bad faith or gross negligence. Such indemnification protection is frequently thought to be desirable, so that individuals who agree to serve in a managerial responsibility and act in furtherance of corporate goals are not held personally responsible for actions which caused harm but were intended to benefit the corporation.

Although many corporations are formed using boilerplate (standardized) bylaws, we believe it is invaluable for the principal shareholders to review the bylaws carefully to make sure the procedures and restrictions which are contained therein are consistent with the way they wish the corporation to operate.

Shareholders' Agreements. Because shares of stock in a corporation are freely transferable (subject to compliance with federal and state securities laws), most shareholders in a family business execute a shareholders' agreement. As more fully discussed in chapter four, a shareholders' agreement can enable the shareholder-owners to restrict the transferability of the shares and thereby help ensure that control of the business remains in the hands of family members. In addition, a shareholders' agreement can be an invaluable mechanism for establishing procedures applicable to governance of the corporation.

MANAGING YOUR CORPORATION

Once your corporation has been formed, it is then managed through a unique system which involves stockholders (shareholders), directors and officers. It is possible (indeed, not unusual in small businesses) for a single person to fill each of these positions. Such overlapping, of course, tends to blur the traditional responsibilities of each position. Understanding the rights and responsibilities of each of these positions is important for at least two reasons. First, if the individual owner(s) of a corporation ignore these positions and their functions, it is more likely that a court of law would find that the limited liability ordinarily afforded shareholders of a corporation should be totally disregarded in a lawsuit against the owners. Second, most corporations do in fact have different individuals filling these different roles. Accordingly, the discussion below seeks to clarify the rights and responsibilities of stockholders, directors and officers.

Stockholders

Stockholders (shareholders) are the owners of a corporation. As owners, they are ultimately responsible for the management of their business, much like U.S. citizens are ultimately responsible for the management of government because they can exercise their vote to elect officials who are responsible for actual decisions. Unlike citizens, who vote for politicians, stockholders vote for directors to serve their corporation. States across the country provide that, with few exceptions, the board of directors are responsible for managing the business of their corporations. The exceptions which give shareholders a more "direct" voice in the management of a corporation are typically limited to extraordinary matters affecting the purpose and/or existence of the corporation, such as an amendment to the articles of incorporation to increase the number of shares of stock which the corporation is authorized to issue; a merger; or a sale of all of the corporation's assets.

A corporation can issue both "voting" and "nonvoting" common stock to its shareholders. Preferred stock is ordinarily nonvoting unless preferred dividends are not paid for a certain period of time or other contractual rights created for the benefit of the preferred holders are violated. Although creating nonvoting stock may be one way of limiting the opportunity for stockholders to exercise any managerial influence over a corporation, most states provide that even nonvoting stockholders can vote on certain major items affecting the corporation. Accordingly, you will want to discuss the rights of nonvoting stockholders with your attorney before creating such a group.

Although the shareholder voting mechanism seems simple — each shareholder has one vote per share to elect directors and vote on certain other major issues — the reality can sometimes be very different. In order to provide a measure of fairness to shareholders who own only a minority interest in a corporation, modern corporation laws recognize such concepts as cumulative voting and class voting. Cumulative voting, for example, gives each shareholder a vote equal to the number of shares he owns multiplied by the number of directors being elected. By "accumulating" this voting power, minority shareholders can sometimes muster enough votes to elect at least one director and so secure board representation. This is important because many corporations (particularly S corporations) are able to distribute their earnings through salaries, interest, rent, etc. and may never need to pay dividends. Minority shareholders who are not represented on the board of directors may, in effect, be "frozen out" of the compensation process if given no managerial authority to help decide *who* gets paid and *how much* they get paid. Accordingly, you must carefully consider how such provisions such as cumulative voting may affect your business and determine whether such provisions should be adopted or rejected.

☞ *STRATEGIC TIP*

Many family members believe that, as stockholders in a family-owned business, they are entitled to a voice in the management of the business. This belief is correct only to the extent that the family members, in their capacity as stockholders, vote on the election of directors and major corporation issues. All other managerial decisions are within the power of the board of directors. This principle allows many business owners to give or sell part of their business away to their family and others without necessarily relinquishing management control. This important concept, while appearing simple, is not always easily understood and can cause severe problems if every stockholder thinks that, as an owner, he has managerial powers over corporate matters which are, in fact, reserved for directors and officers.

Directors

As noted above, the board of directors is given the responsibility of managing a corporation. So great is this responsibility, in fact, that the law generally provides that stockholders have neither the right, power nor authority to dictate to the board how the corporation should be managed. If the shareholders are unhappy with how the directors are managing the business, the remedy is to elect new directors.

The broad duties of the board of directors include:

1. Selecting officers and determining their compensation.
2. Reviewing and approving corporate policies of broad significance, such as expansion of product lines, change in capital structure (new equity and debt, etc.) and public relations.
3. Declaring dividends.
4. Generally providing oversight for the welfare of the corporation as a whole.

Thus, while the stockholders are charged with overseeing major (unusual) changes in the corporation's structure, the board of directors is charged with formulating and overseeing the day-to-day management and policy issues affecting the corporation.

Liability. Because of the potential liability a director can face either to shareholders who claim that the director breached his fiduciary duty or to members of the public who claim to have been injured by actions of the corporation, many individuals (particularly nonowners) are willing to serve as directors only if the corporation provides insurance against such liability. Because the cost of such insurance is high, only large corporations typically provide such protection for their directors.

Procedures. The board of directors ordinarily governs by majority rule. State statutes and/or the bylaws of a corporation regulate when and where the board will meet and how many directors must be present to constitute a quorum to permit director action. Not surprisingly, many disputes have arisen over what one might think to be relatively straightforward matters. Accordingly, the directors must give careful consideration to the "rules of the game" to make sure that their actions and decisions cannot be subsequently challenged for misconstruing or ignoring such procedures.

Directors, like shareholders, can disagree on the management of their corporation. When there is an even number of directors, there is the possibility that a deadlock can occur, half the directors voting one way, the other half voting a contrary way. This problem, discussed in more detail in chapter five, can destroy a corporation. Therefore, consideration should be given to devising some mechanism — such as arbitration — to peacefully resolve the deadlock. One simple solution, of course, is to have an odd number of directors and so preclude the possibility of an even split.

☞ STRATEGIC TIP

Many family businesses have found that they benefit by electing outsiders (i.e., nonfamily members) to the board of directors because they are able to benefit by such directors' experience and insight, yet, at the same time, not necessarily have to relinquish actual ownership in their corporation for such service. Many outsiders are pleased to serve as directors because of the prestige and compensation the position may offer. There is no requirement that directors also be shareholders.

Officers

Although the management of a corporation resides, as noted above, in directors and stockholders, there is a third important group that has managerial authority over business operations. This group, known as officers, is given (or "delegated") authority by the directors. The bylaws of a corporation, among other things, identify the officers of the corporation and define their respective duties. Traditionally, offices include (1) a president, (2) one or more vice-presidents, (3) a secretary, and (4) a treasurer. There is no requirement that officers also be shareholders or directors.

President. Bylaws typically provide that the president shall be the chief executive officer of the corporation and, as such, has responsibility for the general management and control of the business and affairs of the corporation. A president is ordinarily given general supervisory responsibility over all other officers, employees and agents of the corporation.

Vice-President. A vice-president, in addition to having such powers and duties as delegated by the board of directors, may be designated by the board to perform the duties of the president in the event of the president's absence or disability.

Treasurer. A treasurer has general responsibility for maintaining the financial records of the corporation, for disbursing corporate funds as authorized (including dividends), and for preparing (or overseeing preparation by outside accountants) the corporation's financial statements.

Secretary. A secretary is generally responsible for issuing all notices pertaining to meetings of shareholders and directors, for keeping minutes of such meetings, and for maintaining the "corporate books."

☞ *STRATEGIC TIP*

An officer of a corporation has important responsibilities which are conferred by statute, the bylaws and the board of directors. Careful attention should be given to make sure that the individuals with the right talent, judgment and experience fill such positions. Family businesses may be more successful if, while family members remain shareholders and directors, nonfamily members with the right mix of skills are selected to act as corporate officers. Obviously, the selection of nonfamily members to fill the roles of officers may be politically unpalatable to some or all members of the family. In such situations, the family would be wise to agree that family goals (influence, recognition, equality among family members, etc.) should be given priority over business goals (such as profitability, efficiency, etc.).

Chapter Three

Financing Your Family Business

Every business must have a sufficient amount of money to enable it to run from day to day—to purchase supplies; pay salaries; pay the rent; to meet, in short, all of its "operating costs." In addition, most businesses will need money to expand or fund "capital" improvements—a new machine, a new wing of a building, a new delivery truck. Your family business has a better chance of succeeding if it establishes a plan or budget which considers (1) how much money will presently be required to establish the business; (2) how much money will be required in the future to keep the business running; and (3) how much money will be required to provide for desired growth of the business. Once a realistic assessment of these three requirements has been made, a more intelligent decision can be made about what are the most appropriate strategies to raise money for your business.

This chapter considers some of the most common *sources* for obtaining financing to run your business. It then considers the most common *types* of financing such sources provide—loans, equity and loan/equity combinations. Throughout this discussion, we seek to identify the advantages and disadvantages of each of these sources and types of financing. As you will see, you rarely can count on money being supplied "free of charge." Most sources of financing want something in return for providing you with money. Understanding what these things are and how you can structure your arrangement so *you* are satisfied is, perhaps, the most important aspect of this chapter.

YOUR FINANCING REQUIREMENTS

We suggest that one of the first steps you take before actually starting or purchasing your business is to make a detailed list of all of the expenses you can expect to incur in both the short term and long term. In addition, you should prepare a statement of income you reasonably expect your business to generate over the same short and long term. By comparing the summaries of projected expenses and income, you should have a pretty good idea of how much money (1) you would *like* (if possible); (2) you *need* to be comfortable; and (3) would be a bare *minimum* under which amount the business could not be operated. Over the life of your business, its capital requirements will change for a variety of factors such as growth in new areas and an increase in operating expenses (the cost of doing business). Keeping track of the changing needs of your business will help ensure its success.

ALTERNATIVE SOURCES OF FINANCING

The following, singularly or in some combination, are the most common sources of financing which most family businesses consider. Some of the important advantages and disadvantages of these sources of financing are noted.

Personal Resources

One of the most common sources of financing for a new business is the owner's own personal financial resources. Cash savings and many types of personal investments can be easily liquidated and used to buy or rent items required to operate the business.

Advantages. The single biggest advantage to using your own funds is that your business judgments and plans will remain virtually unrestricted. You will not have to explain to anyone (such as an investor who is given stock in "your" business in exchange for his investment) why you are spending or allocating money in one way and not another. In short, there will be no interference with or dilution of your control of the business. Another advantage is that you and your business will not be constrained to repay a third party who advanced funds to your business.

Disadvantages. Use of your own funds may unduly burden your nonbusiness activities and personal budget. Moreover, it may be difficult or impossible to meet the financial requirements of your new business by relying exclusively on your personal resources; few businesses are cheap to set up and operate. Also, many financial advisors suggest it is unwise to put all (or substantially all) of your assets in a single investment. Instead, such advisors suggest that you should diversify your investments to help spread the risk in the event one investment "goes bad." If you have enough confidence in your business plan, the fact that you don't have enough money of your own should not stop you. You can consider the following other sources of financing.

Family, Friends, Personal Acquaintances

Many entrepreneurs approach their family and personal acquaintances to help raise money. Sometimes, acquaintances can refer *their* acquaintances to you. Your professional advisors — attorneys, accountants, bankers, etc. — may know individuals or other businesses who may be interested in investing their money with you. Many "extended family businesses" are often started because parents and children, or sibling and sibling, combine their financial resources in an exciting new venture which is only made possible by the respective financial contributions made by each family member.

Advantages. Some of the above sources may like, love and even trust you, which may result in little or no interference of your control over the business. Also, by comparison to other sources of financing, these sources often require no or relatively simple documentation to reflect their financial commitment, and so may involve minimal legal and accounting expense. Many family businesses, of course, find these advantages to be attractive and, thus, the extended family business is born.

Disadvantages. Perhaps the biggest disadvantages of using family and personal acquaintances as a source of financing are (1) you may be required to prepare appropriate disclosure documents to ensure compliance with federal and state securities laws; (2) personal and family relationships can be strained should the business falter or fail and the investors or lenders lose money; and (3) you may sow the seeds of future dissension as the "closeness" in family relationships dissipates over the generations (i.e., although brothers and sisters may always find a way to work out their differences, their respective grandchildren — second cousins to each other — may be less willing or unable to work out their differences).

Banks and Financial Institutions

Many successful businesses have been able to flourish only as a result of having borrowed money from a bank or other financial institution. Such loans can make the difference between success and failure when a good idea costs more money to implement than the business owner can raise through the sources already identified. This may be particularly true when the business requires a *substantial* amount of money to run efficiently and, perhaps, to grow. For example, you may be unable to purchase a necessary new piece of business equipment which costs $50,000 (or $500,000) without a bank loan. Alternatively, your business may be seasonal and may require a line of credit to carry it through periods of slow sales.

Advantages. Banks and other financial institutions can be sources of a substantial amount of money which can be used to meet your cash-flow and investment requirements. If a bank acts only as a lender, your ownership of the business is not diluted. Rather, the bank is simply a creditor of the business and has only such rights over the control of the business as it may negotiate in its loan documents. For many entrepreneurs, not having to give up an ownership interest in their business makes this financing source more attractive than family and friends, who, perhaps more often, require an ownership interest in a business in exchange for their financial contributions. If that is the case, you may find it preferable to deal with a creditor rather than a co-owner.

Disadvantages. A bank may condition its loan by restricting your business operations through the imposition of "negative covenants." These negative covenants frequently include restrictions on (1) paying dividends; (2) paying salaries above a certain level; (3) incurring additional debt; (4) transferring assets or acquiring additional businesses; and (5) making capital expenditures. A bank may also require a business to meet certain "financial tests" while its loan is outstanding. For example, a bank may insist that a borrower's "debt to equity ratio" remains *below* a certain level or that its ratio of "current assets to current liabilities" remains *above* a certain level. A business which fails to comply with such financial ratios may be required to cure such failure or be threatened with an accelerated payment demand (requiring the outstanding balance of the loan to be paid virtually immediately). A bank may also require shareholders of a corporate borrower to provide personal guarantees (thereby limiting the protection of operating as a corporation). Banks typically do not lend money unless satisfied that the borrower's credit risk is not unduly high, which may require you to submit a detailed business plan, borrowing history, and a statement of your qualifications. Finally, bank financing frequently depends on the existence of sufficient (and demonstrable) cash flow which can be used to repay the loan, as well the existence of sufficient collateral (i.e., cash, inventory, equipment, receivables, real estate, etc.) to repay the loan in the event of a default.

Venture Capital

Many individuals and businesses are in the business of providing "high risk capital" to businesses with an attractive opportunity for growth. Venture capital firms are typically partnerships or corporations which are in the business of making loans to companies with an operating history. Venture capital firms typically make an investment with the hope that the company in which they invest will eventually "go public" by offering the stock on a public stock exchange. Venture capital firms often obtain preferred stock or subordinated debt in exchange for providing a business with funds.

Advantages. Many venture capital firms can provide emerging growth companies not only with money but with business and managerial expertise. For example, venture capital firms can help a business develop a business plan and manage its financial and accounting operations. Venture capital firms can also assist the business in its effort to go public.

Disadvantages. Venture capital firms typically insist on affirmative and negative covenants similar to those demanded by banks. In addition, many venture capital firms require that one or two of their officials serve on the board of directors of the company obtaining the funds. Accordingly, when a business obtains funds from a venture capital firm, it typically relinquishes a considerable amount of autonomy. In addition, since a venture capital firm generally receives equity in exchange for the money it provides, the owner must give up a portion of his ownership in the business to the venture capital firm.

Government Loans/Loan Guarantees

Many volumes have been written on the availability of government financing, especially for small businesses. Although space does not permit a review of the wide variety of financing packages available, we alert you to their existence and urge you to investigate these sources carefully.

Commercial Financing

Finance companies exist which may provide your business with a variety of services, including (1) accounts receivable financing (lending at a discounted rate against your accounts receivable); (2) factoring (selling your accounts receivable at a discounted rate in exchange for financing); and (3) inventory and equipment loans (loans collateralized by your inventory and equipment). Again, we leave to others the important task of discussing this subject in more detail, and simply note here its potential usefulness for your family business.

☞ *STRATEGIC TIP*

In selecting alternative sources of financing, you should carefully consider the following factors: (1) the interest rate offered by each prospective lender; (2) the fees the lender or investor proposes to charge; (3) the degree of control over your business which the lender or investor seeks; and (4) the amount of equity (i.e., ownership interest) the lender or investors seek in your business. By comparing these factors, you can intelligently and rationally select one or more financing sources over other possible sources.

ALTERNATIVE TYPES OF FINANCING

Once a business (or its owner) has identified the source(s) of financing, the type of financing it wants to (or is able to) use must be resolved. A business may obtain financing in one of three principal ways: (1) borrowing money which the business is obligated to repay, together with interest, at specified times (loans or debt financing); (2) obtaining money in exchange for an ownership interest in the business (equity financing); or (3) some combination of debt and equity financing (i.e., debt which can be converted to equity, warrants, options and the like). As we will see, which type(s) of financing a business seeks and obtains will be determined by the availability of the source, the cost of financing, the level of risk of the investment, and the control sought by the lender/investor.

The Debt-Equity Ratio

You should give considerable attention to the question of whether you will raise money for your business by attracting new owners (equity investors) or through loans (debt), or, more likely, in some combination of both. One of the more useful tools that has been developed to help you understand the possible consequences of mixing these various sources of money is the so-called "debt-equity ratio." This is simply a ratio of debt to equity which indicates the extent to which the owners of a business are using their own money as opposed to "outsider loans." Traditionally, many advisors have suggested that a corporation should have more debt than equity ("leverage their business with debt") because (1) interest payable on debt is tax deductible; (2) the funds provided by the debt financing can be put to use by the borrower which yields higher returns to the borrower than the cost to the borrower of the loan.

☞ *STRATEGIC TIP*

As the national and world economy has suffered in recent years, more and more businesses have revised their optimum debt-equity ratio to become less dependent on debt. Many businesses believe that it is preferable not to take on too much debt initially so they can arrange for additional debt financing if and when the growth or survival of their business is at stake. Also, the consequence of not paying a dividend may be to have unhappy shareholders, while the consequence of not paying a lender may be to risk a foreclosure action.

Financing Your Business With Debt

Although debt takes many forms, it generally reflects a contractual obligation of a borrower (the "debtor") to repay money loaned by the bank, finance company or other lender (the "creditor"), together with interest at an agreed-upon level (which may be "fixed" or "variable"). A creditor who loans money to a business does not, by virtue of the loan, obtain an ownership interest in the business. Rather, the creditor typically obtains the contractual obligation of the business to repay the loan. The most important terms in a debt financing relate to (1) when payment of principal and interest is required; (2) the rate of interest to be paid; and (3) events that will entitle the lender to accelerate repayment of the loan and pursue collection remedies. In the event a business defaults on its repayment obligation and goes into bankruptcy, it generally must pay its creditors before it makes any payments to its shareholders.

Advantages. The biggest advantages associated with the use of debt financing are: (1) it provides the borrower with money without causing a dilution in the ownership of the borrower; and (2) debt provides the opportunity for "leverage"—using other people's money to create financial opportunity for yourself. In addition, the interest expense paid on borrowed money (unlike dividends paid to shareholders) is deductible. So, from a tax perspective, debt financing has certain advantages over equity financing.

Disadvantages. Perhaps the biggest disadvantage of debt is its inflexibility: The borrower is obligated to repay principal and interest at stated times regardless of the level of income the business is generating. If the business fails to repay the debt, ownership of the business could be lost upon foreclosure by the lender. Other disadvantages may include the difficulty some businesses (without track records) face in their efforts to obtain debt financing. Another disadvantage is that lenders commonly restrict the borrower's operating freedom by imposing affirmative and negative covenants on the borrower.

☞ *STRATEGIC TIP*

It is possible for a business to borrow money from more than one source. In that event, decisions must be made (typically on the basis of bargaining strength) as to which loan(s) have priority over which other loan(s) in the event the business cannot pay all of the loans in full. Subordination agreements are often used to specify which loans have priority and which loans are "subordinated" to other loans. Creative financing techniques relying on such subordination agreements may be available to help protect some (but not all) family members who may require greater protection from risk than other family members. In addition, in exchange for their lower priority, subordinated lenders (including any family members who are lenders) generally insist upon a higher yield or rate of return than do senior debt holders.

Types of Debt

Debt can be structured in a virtually infinite variety of ways. Some of the more common types of debt include:

Trade Credit. Strictly speaking, trade credit is not indebtedness for borrowed money. Rather, it is the liability a business incurs to its suppliers for products supplied to the business or services rendered to the business. For example, Acme Publishing may deliver 1,000 editions of a new book to Owl Bookstores on the condition that Owl pays the invoice for the books within forty-five days following the date the books are delivered. During such forty-five-day period, Owl has use of the money it will soon be obligated to pay to Acme.

☞ STRATEGIC TIP

If a family owns more than one business, it is possible for one business to extend trade credit to another. In order to ensure that each business retains its separate legal identity, it is important that such trade debt be repaid by the business incurring the liability. Also, the forgiveness of such debt may result in the unintended imposition of a tax. Accordingly, families doing business with each other should generally deal with each other as they would with other businesses.

Promissory Notes. Short-term debt (i.e., debt which must be repaid in one year or less) is often evidenced or documented by a "promissory note" or "note." Notes are often executed in connection with a loan agreement which may, among other things, restrict management compensation, the payment of dividends, new investments, etc. A note need be no more elaborate than a piece of paper in which the borrower simply agrees to repay a stated amount of money at a stated time or on demand of the creditor.

☞ STRATEGIC TIP

In order to avoid the unintended imposition of taxes, intrafamily loans should be reflected by notes or other suitable instruments and repaid in accordance with their terms.

Bonds, Debentures and Mortgages. Longer-term debt obligations are ordinarily reflected by one of three types of instruments: (1) *bonds* which are long-term debt typically "secured" by the borrower's real property; (2) *debentures* which are long-term debt that is unsecured; and (3) *mortgages* which, strictly speaking, are not a form of debt but, rather, an encumbrance on a borrower's real property (land and buildings) given to secure a borrower's repayment obligation. Many bond issues are also secured by mortgages on real property.

☞ *STRATEGIC TIP*

Certain family businesses are sufficiently well established that they can arrange to issue bonds to members of the public. Bonds are simply long-term repayment obligations of the "issuer" (i.e., the business borrowing money). The issuer of bonds may be able to pay a lower interest rate on its borrowing if no one single creditor (or bondholder) holds all of the bonds, because no one single creditor will be assuming the entire risk associated with the borrowing. During periods when interest rates are expected to increase, the corporate issuer may benefit by borrowing at the current rate in the expectation that it will be able to earn a higher return on its investment in the borrowed funds. Since bonds typically carry no voting rights, issuing bonds generally does not (in the absence of a default on payment) alter voting control of a business.

Term Loan. A term loan is a loan made in a lump sum (or fixed amount) that is repayable on a fixed date or dates. For example, a bank may loan Owl Bookstore $500,000 on January 1, 1993 on the condition that Owl Bookstore repays this amount, together with interest, in ten equal annual installments. Depending on your bargaining power, you may be able to reduce the amount of interest charged and/or extend the time you have to repay the loan. Generally, if the term of a loan is in excess of one year, the lender will insist on obtaining a "security interest" in the assets of the business, including inventory, equipment, receivables, etc., and a mortgage on the real estate of the business. The term loan may also be secured by a lien or mortgage on the assets of the principal shareholder(s) of the borrower and/or a personal guarantee of the principal shareholder(s) of the borrower. Such security interests help protect certain lenders by giving them the right to specific property (or the proceeds from a sale of such property) to satisfy their debt before other (general) creditors are repaid. Businesses typically use term loans to finance capital improvements or provide working capital.

Revolving Line of Credit. In a revolving line of credit, a bank or other institutional lender agrees to loan a borrower up to a maximum dollar amount for a specified period of time. The borrower may draw on (or borrow against) the line of credit from time to time and make periodic repayments from time to time. The repayments increase or replenish the borrowing availability under the line of credit. For example, a bank may extend a $500,000, five-year, revolving line of credit to Owl Bookstore. Owl may borrow $100,000 in year one, repay a portion of this amount at the beginning of year two and borrow again later in year two. As long as Owl does not exceed the $500,000 limit, it can continue to borrow and repay money from the bank for the period of the loan. Generally, the amount of money a bank will extend to a borrower in a revolving loan will depend on the level of existing collateral (*e.g.*, inventory and accounts receivables) that the business has pledged in favor of the bank. A revolving line of credit is typically used to provide working capital to a business.

Financing Your Business With Equity

Equity, like debt, may take many forms (e.g., common stock, preferred stock, convertible preferred stock, partnership interests, etc.). Unlike the incurrence of debt, the issuance of equity confers an ownership interest in the investor. Whereas the holder of debt is contractually entitled to receive repayment of its loan at a stated time or times and in specified amounts, the holder of equity will generally enjoy a return on his investment only if he sells his interest to another investor, the business declares a dividend on its stock or partnership interests, or the business is merged or liquidated. If a business is liquidated, the shareholders or partners will be entitled to all of the assets of the business in accordance with their respective ownership interests, but only after all of the debts and other liabilities of the business (e.g., bank loans, subordinated debt financings, taxes, trade credits, accrued wages, etc.) have been paid or discharged.

Advantages. Equity financing (such as the issuance of common stock in a corporation) may be the only type of financing available to many new businesses. There may be some important advantages arising out of financing through equity. For example, the more equity that is contributed to the business, the easier it will become to secure debt financing in the future. Another advantage of raising money by issuing equity is that the business will not be under any obligation to make a fixed repayment on the equity. Dividends are payable only at the discretion of the board of directors of the company. Accordingly, the issuance of equity does not place a burden on the cash flow of the company.

Disadvantages. Unlike debt holders, equity holders (except preferred shareholders) have no assurance that they will receive a return on their investment. The business is not obligated to repay the owner/investor's equity contribution nor is it obligated to pay dividends or make other distributions (until the liquidation of the business, at which time net assets are distributed among shareholders in accordance with their percentage interests). The claims of equity holders are also subordinated to the claims of company creditors and preferred shareholders. Accordingly, in the event of bankruptcy or liquidation, equity holders will be the last group to be "repaid." A significant disadvantage of raising money by issuing equity is the dilution in percentage ownership experienced by existing investors. Assume, for example, that Owl Bookstore has five shareholders who each own 200 shares of stock. If Owl issues an additional 1,000 shares of stock to a new investor in exchange for a $500,000 investment, the percentage ownership of each of the five original shareholders will decline from 20 percent to 10 percent. This dilution in ownership may be acceptable, of course, especially if the new investor is paying more per share than the original investors paid for their shares.

PRACTICAL ASPECTS OF RAISING MONEY

Once a business determines the level of capital (i.e., money) it requires, it must decide whether to raise that capital by borrowing money, by issuing equity, or through a combination of the two.

If the business borrows money, it will be obligated to repay the loan out of its cash flow on specific dates. For some businesses, a fixed repayment obligation may be burdensome. If the business fails to meet its repayment obligations, the creditor can sue to recover the money owed to it and seize assets of the business to satisfy its debt. Moreover, because creditors typically insist on subjecting the borrower to more extensive contractual restrictions during the term of the loan than do equity holders, a borrower should be prepared for a diminution in its authority to control the business.

Although a business, by issuing equity, can avoid the fixed-payment obligation (and, to some extent, the contractual operating restrictions) which debt entails, the issuance of equity will dilute the existing equity holders' ownership interest in the business. By adding new equity holders, the original equity holders lose a portion of their control over the business.

The Cost of Financing

The interest rate that a business must pay on money loaned to it, or the percentage of equity it must give the investor in exchange for money invested in it, will depend largely on the financial condition and prospects of the business. The weaker the business, the higher the interest rate it must pay on a loan in order to compensate the lender for the increased risk. For example, if a lender charges an established business that is considered highly unlikely to default on a loan an interest rate of 10 percent per annum, the lender will charge a borrower it believes is a higher credit risk a higher interest rate to compensate for the additional risk it assumes in making the loan. Similarly, the weaker the business or the dimmer its prospects for success, the greater the percentage of equity which must be issued to an investor in exchange for a fixed dollar amount in order to compensate the investor for the increased risk.

☞ *STRATEGIC TIP*

It is desirable to determine the minimum amount of money your business needs today and the amount of money your business may need in the future. If your business proves successful, you may be able to raise additional money in the future at a lower cost than the money you raise today!

A number of approaches are available to a business to reduce the cost of raising money through debt and equity financing. The following approaches are not meant to be exhaustive, nor will all such approaches necessarily be available to your business. We believe, however, that you will be better able to negotiate the optimal financing package for your business if you are aware of these approaches to reducing the cost of raising money.

Reducing the Cost of Debt

Approaches to reducing the cost of raising money through debt financing include:

Security Interests. Debt is characterized as either "secured debt" or "unsecured debt." A creditor may secure a debt by taking a mortgage in the debtor's real estate and/or a security interest under the Uniform Commercial Code in the debtor's personal property (e.g., inventory, accounts receivable, motor vehicles, patents, trademarks, equipment and the like). In the event that a debtor fails to repay the loan of a creditor holding a mortgage or security interest, the creditor, by following certain legal procedures, will be entitled to seize the specific assets in which it has a mortgage or security interest and use the proceeds from the sale of these assets to pay off its loan. If the debtor has granted a mortgage or security interest in the same assets to more than one secured creditor, specific rules of law govern which of the mortgages or security interests will have "priority" in the covered assets in the event that the debtor defaults and the secured creditors look to the same assets to be repaid. Frequently, a secured creditor will restrict the debtor's ability to grant additional security interests in assets in favor of subsequent creditors.

Unsecured Creditors. If a creditor does not obtain a mortgage or security interest in assets of the debtor, the creditor will be an unsecured creditor. In the event that the debtor defaults in repayment of its loan, the unsecured creditor will only receive repayment of its loan out of the assets of the debtor that remain after all assets in which secured creditors have mortgages and security interests have been liquidated to pay off the debts held by the secured creditors.

☞ *STRATEGIC TIP*

(Consider Providing Security Interests)

Because a secured creditor has priority over unsecured creditors if your business cannot repay its debts, the creditor who takes a mortgage or security interest in your business' assets will face less risk than a junior secured creditor (e.g., the holder of a second mortgage) or the holder of an unsecured debt. Accordingly, a secured creditor ordinarily is prepared to accept a lower interest rate on a loan than is the junior secured creditor or the unsecured creditor. Therefore, one way for your business to reduce the "cost of borrowing" is by granting the lender a mortgage or security interest in specific assets.

Personal Guarantee. A debtor that is unable to borrow money at an affordable interest rate may be able to reduce its borrowing costs if a more credit-worthy person or entity guarantees the debtor's repayment obligation. Like the "primary" obligation of the debtor, the guarantor's obligation may be either secured or unsecured. Letters of credit are occasionally used to accomplish the same purpose as a guarantee: to provide the backing of a more credit-worthy person behind the obligation of a debtor. Letters of credit are issued by banks and permit the creditor-beneficiary to draw on or get an advance of money under the letter in the event that the primary debtor defaults on its repayment obligation.

Whether it makes sense for a debtor to obtain a third-party guarantee of a loan depends on whether the cost of the guarantee is less than the savings that will be achieved through the reduced interest rate of a guaranteed loan.

☞ *STRATEGIC TIP*

Many people mistakenly assume that if they form a corporation through which to conduct business activities, they will simply be able to walk away from any financial liabilities their business has incurred if the business fails. In fact, banks, landlords and suppliers, recognizing that a corporation provides limited liability for its shareholders, will frequently insist that one or more of the shareholders guarantee the obligations of the corporation under the loan, lease or supply contract. By giving such a guarantee, the shareholder becomes personally liable for the corporate obligation he is guaranteeing.

Opportunity to Convert Debt to Equity. Unlike owners of a business, who stand to profit if their business prospers and increases in value, the lender does not participate in the "upside potential" of a business. The lender will simply receive repayment of the principal amount of its loan plus interest. If, however, the lender can convert its debt into equity, the lender will have the ability to share in the appreciation of the business' value. Lenders who are afforded the opportunity to share in the upside potential of a business typically charge a lower interest rate on their loans than do lenders who are not given such a right.

Therefore, a third way to reduce the cost of borrowing money is by giving the lender a right to convert some or all of its loan into equity in your business. If you do provide such a conversion right to the lender, you should be careful to negotiate an acceptable "conversion ratio" to ensure that the lender does not receive a disproportionate share of the equity in your business upon conversion of its loan.

Adjustable Interest Rates. A lender who makes a long-term loan to a business at a fixed interest rate will see the value of its loan decline if the general level of interest rates rises over the term of the loan. For example, a lender who is stuck with a ten-year loan at a 7 percent interest rate has made a bad deal if the market rate of interest rises to 10 percent during this period. As a safeguard against this possibility, a fixed-rate lender ordinarily provides itself with a "cushion" to protect itself in the event that interest rates rise. You may be able to avoid this interest cushion cost by agreeing to pay your lender at an interest rate that "floats" (up or down) with the market rate of interest.

☞ *STRATEGIC TIP*

Although borrowing at a floating interest rate will enable your business to avoid paying the fixed interest rate loan "premium" and will also enable your business to benefit from a decline in interest rates, borrowing at a floating rate risks an increased expense in the event that interest rates float *higher* than you anticipated. You might want to agree with the lender to cap the level at which a loan will bear interest to limit your maximum exposure. Such a cap may limit the maximum increase in the interest rate from year to year as well as over the life of the loan.

Subordination. If a business needs to borrow money at a time when it already has debt outstanding, the prospective lender may be willing to charge a lower interest rate if the existing lender agrees to subordinate its loan to the new loan. Although subordination agreements come in a variety of forms, they generally provide that, as between the senior and junior creditor, the senior creditor is entitled to payment before the junior creditor in the event that the debtor has insufficient funds to pay principal and interest on both of its loans. Some subordination agreements restrict the ability of the debtor to repay the junior creditor any amount until the senior creditor has been repaid in full.

☞ *STRATEGIC TIP*

Depending on the financial resources and requirements of family members who have loaned the business money, it may be desirable to subordinate some family member loans to others in exchange for varying rates of returns.

"Tailor-Made" Contractual Agreements. Because debt represents a contractual obligation by the debtor to repay the creditor, these parties may, through negotiation, establish a variety of contractual agreements for the repayment of the debt that best suits their respective needs. For example, a business may not be in a financial position to pay a fixed amount of interest every month or even every year after it has incurred the debt because its cash flow is too unpredictable or small. However, both the creditor and the debtor may reasonably believe that within ten years the business will have matured to the point where its cash flow will be strong and predictable. In such a situation, the creditor and debtor could agree upon a repayment schedule pursuant to which the debtor would not be obligated to pay any interest on the loan during the first ten years following the date of the loan but would, on the tenth anniversary of the loan, be required to repay not only the principal amount of the loan but also an amount representing the interest that has accrued but not been paid on the loan. A loan whose principal all comes due on a single date is sometimes referred to as a "bullet" loan.

Reducing the Cost of Equity

Approaches to reducing the cost of raising money through equity financing include:

Provide a Liquidation Preference. In the event that a business is terminated, the assets remaining after all debts and liabilities of the business have been paid or provided for will ordinarily be distributed to the shareholders in accordance with their percentage ownership interests. If a class of shareholders has been contractually granted a "preference" over another class of shareholders to some or all of the assets of the business upon its liquidation, purchasers of this preferred class of shares are ordinarily prepared to pay a higher price for their shares than they would pay if they were not promised a liquidation preference. Therefore, one way for your corporation to reduce its cost of issuing equity is by issuing a class of preferred stock that has a liquidation preference. For example, a class of preferred stock may be issued with a $100 liquidation preference. In the event that the corporation is liquidated, each holder of a share of preferred stock would be entitled to receive $100 before any distributions could be made to holders of common stock or other classes of equity that do not have a liquidation preference.

☞ *STRATEGIC TIP*

The articles of incorporation must set forth the terms and conditions of the "preferences" attached to each class of stock. The articles should state whether the owners of preferred stock are entitled to share (on one basis or another) with owners of the common stock in the residual assets of the corporation which remain after the preferred stockholders have received their preferential distribution. The articles can also provide that the preferred stockholders' preferential distribution is their sole payment upon liquidation of the corporation.

Pay Dividends in Fixed Amounts at Regular Intervals. Whereas interest on debt is due and payable at stated times and in stated amounts, the articles of incorporation for most corporations provide that stock dividends are generally payable only if and when declared by the board of directors. However, it is possible for a corporation to issue a class of stock that pays dividends in fixed amounts on fixed dates. Such mandatory dividend payments are analogous to fixed-interest payments. An investor who knows that he will receive fixed dividend payments will be willing to pay a higher price for a share of stock than an investor who is not assured a dividend payment.

☞ *STRATEGIC TIP*

The lack of a contractual entitlement to dividends typically makes an investment riskier and, so, more expensive. If the risk can be removed, the investment (equity) may become cheaper. Therefore, a second approach to reducing the cost of equity financing may be to issue stock in your corporation which pays a fixed dividend. If your corporation pays a sufficiently high fixed dividend, it should be able to obtain a higher price for its stock.

Mix Preferred Stock and Debt. Equity in the form of preferred stock that (1) pays a fixed dividend, (2) has a stated liquidation preference, and (3) is subject to mandatory redemption (i.e., "repurchase") by the issuing corporation on a stated date has characteristics similar to debt. The preferred stock and debt both entitle the holder to a fixed return on a scheduled date, while neither affords the holder the right to benefit if the business appreciates in value. Preferred stock and debt differ, however, in two fundamental ways. First, preferred stock dividends are generally not tax deductible by the corporation, whereas a corporation is permitted to deduct the interest payments it makes on its debt. Accordingly, the use of debt can provide substantial tax advantages over the use of equity. Second, in the event of a corporation's bankruptcy, the holder of the debt would fare better than the holder of preferred stock since the bankruptcy law affords holders of debt a superior claim to the assets of the corporation. In other words, if the assets of the corporation are insufficient to repay both the debt of the corporation and the liquidation preference on the preferred stock, the debt will be paid in its entirety before any payments are made on account of the preferred stock.

☞ STRATEGIC TIP

Because the characteristics of debt and equity can be shaped in a wide variety of ways, it may be useful for your family business to examine the merits of using one or the other financing form in order to determine whether business objectives can be reached through a careful shaping of the characteristics of the debt and equity it issues.

☞ STRATEGIC TIP

Because of the complexity of the tax law, it is essential that you consult with your attorney before creating one or more classes of preferred stock in order to confirm that the Internal Revenue Service will, in fact, treat the preferred stock as equity rather than as debt.

Give Certain Shareholders a "Put Option." Unlike debt, which matures and is to be repaid at a specified time, equity represents the ownership of the business and shares of a corporation theoretically may be held by the shareholders indefinitely. However, because people in the real world do not hold their shares indefinitely, business owners want to have the opportunity to sell or otherwise dispose of their ownership interests. If a broad or public market has developed for the stock of a corporation, the owner will be able to sell his stock to another investor in the marketplace. If, as is typical in many family businesses, there is not a "public market" for the stock of the corporation, it may be difficult or impossible for an owner to find a buyer to purchase his stock at a reasonable price. Accordingly, a potential investor in a business whose stock is not widely traded may be more willing to invest (or pay a higher price for the stock at the time he makes his investment) if he is afforded the right to "put" (or sell) the stock to the issuing corporation (or another of its shareholders) at an agreed-upon price and date and/or upon other agreed circumstances.

Because there is generally no open market to buy and sell shares in a family-owned business, many potential investors may choose not to invest in such a business because they are afraid of being "stuck" if they ever reach an irreconcilable difference with the majority owner(s). By providing such "outside" investors with a contractual right to sell their shares to family shareholders (or the corporation itself), it may be easier to attract these investors.

Your corporation (or other person obligated to buy the shareholder's stock in the event the put right is exercised) should consider reaching agreement with the shareholder on the precise time and the circumstances in which the put may be exercised. Such an agreement may help avoid an unexpected obligation to pay the put price for such stock. Also, to help ensure sufficient cash flow to pay for the shares being put, your corporation or the party purchasing the shares may seek an agreement to pay the put price (together with interest) over a period of time after the put has been exercised.

LEGAL ASPECTS OF RAISING MONEY

No discussion on business financing would be complete without some consideration of the various federal and state laws which have developed over the years to regulate raising money through either equity or debt financing. Because documents or "instruments" which evidence various forms of equity and debt financing are known as "securities," this area of the law is known, not surprisingly, as "securities law."

When most of us think of securities laws and the Securities and Exchange Commission (the SEC), we think of large public companies such as Exxon or General Motors. We may think of insider trading and the scandals on Wall Street during the 1980s when Ivan Boesky, Dennis Levine and Michael Milken became household names. We may not think that securities laws have any applicability to family businesses, other than, perhaps, to the largest of family businesses. In fact, however, securities laws are applicable to all businesses that raise money through debt or equity financing. Therefore, you should review the applicability of such laws with your attorney in the event your business pursues such financing.

Federal Securities Law

Transactions in securities fall into two general categories: (1) the initial issuance of securities by a corporation, partnership or other business entity (commonly referred to as the "issuer" of the securities) and (2) subsequent trading in the securities by the persons who invested in them. A comprehensive and complicated set of federal and state securities laws regulate both the *initial issuance* of securities and *subsequent trading* in the securities.

Securities Act of 1933

The principal federal statute regulating the initial issuance of securities is the Securities Act of 1933 (the "1933 Act"). This statute is designed to ensure that the issuer of securities provides adequate (i.e., "full and fair") disclosure of material information to purchasers at the time it offers and sells securities to them. Thus this statute seeks to prevent fraud in the offer and sale of securities.

Securities Exchange Act of 1934

The principal federal statute regulating *trading* in securities is the Securities Exchange Act of 1934 (the "1934 Act"). This statute prohibits fraud and manipulation in the trading of securities, regulates securities brokers and dealers and requires the filing of numerous reports pertaining to securities ownership with the SEC. The 1934 Act is generally relevant only to large family businesses that have raised a substantial amount of money by issuing securities to the public. In contrast, the 1933 Act is applicable to any family business—whether a partnership or a corporation—that seeks to raise money from even one or two outside investors.

The SEC administers the federal securities laws, including the 1933 Act and the 1934 Act. The SEC has promulgated numerous regulations under each of these statutes. In order to comply with the securities laws, these statutes and the administrative regulations promulgated by the SEC under its broad rule-making powers must be understood. The following discussion is intended to provide a broad and useful overview of federal securities laws which should prompt and facilitate further discussion with your attorney.

Regulating the Issuance of Securities

Any time a business (or "issuer") seeks to raise money by issuing debt or equity securities, it must first determine whether the money-raising transaction involves the issuance of securities. The term "security," as defined in the 1933 Act, has been broadly construed by the courts to include the property interest which an investor receives in exchange for an investment of money with the expectation of profit to be derived largely from the efforts of others. A security has been defined to include common stock, preferred stock, bonds, stock options and similar types of instruments. The term security has also been construed to include less conventional approaches to raising money. For example, membership interests in an investment club have been found to constitute securities where each member invests money in the club in order to earn profits from an investment advisor's efforts. Courts have been confronted with hundreds of cases questioning whether a particular type of investment constitutes a security, and anyone seeking to determine whether a novel form of investment constitutes a security will need to make an evaluation in light of the precedent found in these cases.

☞ STRATEGIC TIP

It is generally safe to assume that whenever a family business seeks to raise money by issuing common or preferred stock, even to family members, close friends or valued employees, the business is issuing a security. Even if only a small amount of money is sought in exchange for stock, the stock sold will constitute a security because there is no minimum dollar amount required by law before stock will be considered a security.

Registration

Any time a security is offered for sale, either the offer and sale must be registered under applicable securities laws (i.e., the 1933 Act and the state "blue-sky" laws where the investors are located) or an exemption from the registration requirements must exist.

In order to register securities, a registration statement must be prepared which discloses the issuer's historical and current activities and financial condition so that prospective investors have necessary information to enable them to make an informed investment decision. Registration statements must also contain information on the background of the issuer's directors, executive officers and significant shareholders.

The cost of preparing a registration statement is extremely high (often exceeding $100,000) because the required disclosure necessitates substantial involvement of the issuer's attorney and accountant. In order to avoid the time and expense of preparing a registration statement (as well as the potential liability of an issuer, its directors and officers if the registration statement misstates or omits material information), issuers will generally prefer to issue securities in a manner which "exempts" them from the registration requirements. Fortunately, most family businesses are able to rely on an available exemption and so avoid the registration requirements. The following section discusses one of the most important exemptions to the registration requirement.

Exemption From Registration. The most commonly relied upon exemption from the registration requirements of the securities laws is the "private placement." A private placement is generally characterized by the absence of general advertisement of the issuer's securities and by the presence of a small number of investors. Federal and state regulations provide specific guidelines which enable the issuer to know with reasonable certainty that its issuance of securities complies with the private placement exemption from the registration requirements. Certain of these guidelines relate to the number of purchasers involved in the offering and others relate to the amount of money which an issuer seeks to raise in its offering. One guideline, for example, permits an issuer to sell its securities in a single offering to up to thirty-five people without having to comply with the registration requirements. These guidelines provide that certain "accredited investors" who meet established financial tests do not count against the thirty-five-person limitation. Many family businesses raise money (often inadvertently) under the private placement exemption. We suggest that you discuss this exemption with your attorney.

Antifraud Provisions

Even if securities are issued under an exemption from the registration requirements, the securities laws still require compliance with "antifraud" provisions. Accordingly, great care must be taken to ensure that any statements which are made by (or on behalf of) a business in connection with its issuance of securities neither misstates (nor omits to state) a material fact. Violations of these antifraud provisions can result in the imposition of severe civil and criminal penalties on the parties responsible for the misstatements and/or omissions.

☞ *STRATEGIC TIP*

A family business seeking to raise money by issuing common stock will frequently prepare a brief disclosure document, commonly referred to as a "private placement memorandum," which discloses the nature of the business, strategy for future activities, the expected use of the proceeds raised from the securities offering, and the material risks associated with the offering. In addition, the business may afford prospective investors the opportunity to ask appropriate questions of senior management. A family business which is contemplating the issuance of securities in order to raise money should involve legal counsel as early in the process as possible. Early involvement of counsel will help the business avoid missteps which could entail liability, delay and embarrassment.

Securities Trading

As mentioned earlier, trading in securities that have already been issued is subject to extensive regulation by the securities laws. Just because the issuer of securities has validly issued the securities does *not* mean that the investor in the securities is free to resell them. In fact, when securities are sold by an issuer pursuant to an exemption from the registration requirements, the securities constitute "restricted securities" and generally may not be resold for at least three years, absent unusual circumstances.

☞ *STRATEGIC TIP*

The SEC has promulgated a safe-harbor rule for the resale of restricted securities. The safe-harbor is known as Rule 144. Before you allow anyone who has purchased restricted securities in your family business to resell them, consult your legal advisor to make sure that the securities can be resold under Rule 144 or another exemption. The rules and regulations in this area are particularly complex.

Antifraud Provisions and Insider Trading

Rule 10b-5 of the 1934 Act makes it unlawful for any person to engage in any practice which would operate as a fraud upon another person in connection with the purchase or sale of a security. The prohibition contained in Rule 10b-5 applies to trading in securities on the public stock markets and to privately negotiated purchases and sales. Essentially, "insiders" of a business may not engage in purchases and sales of securities issued by their business without first disclosing all material information pertaining to the corporation to the purchaser. Failure of an insider to adhere to this "disclose or abstain" rule can lead to serious securities law problems for the insider. In addition, a person (who may or may not be an insider) who "leaks" material inside information to another person can be held liable under the antifraud provisions of the securities laws if the "beneficiary" of the leaked information uses that information to trade in the securities.

Penalties for Violations. Persons who violate the insider trading prohibitions of the federal securities laws face civil damages and criminal penalties. The civil damages can consist of disgorgement of the profits earned as a result of the fraudulent conduct and a fine in excess of the profit gained or financial loss avoided. The criminal penalties can consist of monetary fines and imprisonment. In addition, the SEC can seek a civil penalty against a company and, possibly, its directors and supervisory personnel as "controlling persons" for failure to take appropriate steps to prevent illegal trading. Finally, the mere appearance of impropriety under the securities laws could damage a company's reputation for integrity and impair investor confidence in the company.

☞ *STRATEGIC TIP*

Your company may wish to consider adopting a formal policy that no employee, regardless of his position within the company, may purchase or sell the company's securities while in the possession of material inside information concerning the company. This prohibition typically affects all employees who have access to material nonpublic information about the company.

There may occasionally be material nonpublic information within your company that is not yet ripe for public disclosure. For example, negotiations regarding a new business or product acquisition may be too tentative to require, or even permit, public announcement by your company. On the other hand, the information may be quite material in the sense that individuals with access to the information are themselves precluded from trading in the company's securities. Whenever any doubt exists, the presumption should be against insider trading in your company's securities until you or other insiders have consulted with an attorney to confirm that such trading is not inappropriate under the circumstances.

State Blue-Sky Laws

As indicated earlier, the issuer of securities must comply not only with the federal securities laws (the 1933 Act and 1934 Act) but with the securities laws (known as blue-sky laws) of the states where the investors reside. The blue-sky laws are not uniform; they vary from state to state. It is not unusual for a company to determine not to sell securities in a particular state in order to avoid the need to comply with the securities laws of such state.

Owl Bookstore

Let's assume that Owl Bookstore wishes to raise $500,000 to pay for an expansion of its facilities. The owner, John Smith, has five friends who are each willing to invest $100,000 in the business. What are the questions that must be addressed?

First, in exchange for their investments, what will the five friends receive? Assuming they receive common stock, how many shares will they be issued? The answer to this question depends on the value of the business and the number of shares of common stock that will be outstanding following the issuance of shares to the investors.

Second, is there an exemption from the registration requirements imposed by the 1933 Act? The answer to this question should be "yes." The 1933 Act exempts from the registration requirements a "private placement" of securities. If, however, Owl Bookstore were seeking to raise $6,000,000 for nationwide expansion and engaged an investment banking firm to find buyers among the general public interested in investing in Owl, the private placement exemption might not be available. The availability of an exemption from the registration requirements of the 1933 Act involves a case-by-case analysis.

Third, even if the offer and sale of securities to the five friends of John Smith are exempt from registration under the 1933 Act, will the offer and sale be exempt under state blue-sky laws? If two of the friends live in Connecticut and three of the friends live in New York, Smith and his attorney must review both Connecticut and New York laws to confirm that an exemption from the state registration requirements is available. Often, an exemption is available as long as an appropriate notice is filed with the applicable state securities commissioner.

Fourth, must Owl Bookstore provide the investors, all friends of John Smith, with information relating to the activities of Owl and the proposed investment? More often than not, the answer is "yes." The securities laws generally require that basic information relating to the issuer and the terms of the investment be disclosed to investors. If, for example, John Smith tells his friends that Owl is earning $100,000 per year and assures them that Owl's prospects for the future are bright, he faces serious problems if, in fact, he knows that three well-known bookstore chains are scheduled to open up new bookstores within two blocks of Owl's main location. The securities laws are designed, in short, to protect investors against misleading statements and the omission of material information in connection with the offer and sale of securities.

Fifth, if Owl sells common stock to five friends of Smith, will these investors be able to freely resell the common stock they acquired or will their ability to resell such stock be restricted by the securities laws? Generally, the investors who purchase securities in a private placement will not be able to resell such securities until a significant period of time (perhaps as long as three years) has elapsed from the date of their investment. Moreover, transfer of the securities may be restricted by a shareholders' agreement.

CONCLUSION

The foregoing discussion is intended to be a simplified but useful summary of the sometimes complex mechanisms which may be available to help you raise money for your business. Because of the complexity of this subject, we recommend that you seek specific advice about the particular circumstances facing *your* family business before proceeding to attempt to raise money.

Chapter Four

Agreements Among Owners

I f you are — and always will be — the sole owner of your business, you may wish to skip this (and the next) chapter. If, however, you have — or expect to have — one or more co-owners (such as a parent, child or sibling), this (and the next) chapter should be carefully read. The subjects of these chapters are particularly important for family businesses with more than one owner because, with planning, you and your co-owners have an opportunity to agree — at a time when there may be little or no stress — on how to handle potentially stressful or unpleasant conflicts that ordinarily arise over the course of time in any business. The subjects of these chapters may also help to reduce or eliminate such conflicts. If such planning is not undertaken, the law of your particular state will impose its own particular solution to the conflict or situation you face. Through advance planning, you can, perhaps, reach a more satisfactory (and less expensive) solution than the law would otherwise provide. In addition, it is usually easier to plan your personal life if you know that certain issues have been resolved today rather than deferred to a later day. The subjects discussed in this chapter are designed, in short, to help you avoid the subject of the next chapter — what happens in the event of a dispute or disagreement with your co-owners.

PARTNERSHIP AGREEMENTS

As noted in the first two chapters, a general partnership can be formed with virtually no formality. If two or more persons or businesses join forces to work together for profit, a partnership may exist under state law. Even the simplest of partnership ventures, however, will inevitably present questions which need to be resolved. For example, if the partners have an opportunity to pursue a significant business opportunity (such as buying a new bookstore) but pursuit of such opportunity will require additional funds, can the partners be forced to contribute additional funds and what are the consequences if they do not? Many partners find it desirable to address a variety of issues in a written partnership agreement before actually commencing partnership operations in order to assist their planning, to avoid uncertainty, and to limit the likelihood of grounds for reasonable dispute.

The first step in preparing a written partnership agreement is for the partners to reach an understanding as to their objectives in running and managing the business, including how partnership profits and losses are to be allocated among the partners. We suggest that, at a minimum, you address the following basic areas in your written partnership agreement:

Management of the Partnership

In the absence of an agreement to the contrary, every partner is an agent of the partnership and has the authority to bind the partnership. By law in some states, certain "extraordinary" decisions may require unanimous consent by the partners. For example, the Delaware Uniform Partnership Law provides:

Unless authorized by the other partners or unless they have abandoned the business, one or more but less than all the partners have no authority to:

1. Assign the partnership property in trust for creditors or on the assignee's promise to pay debts of the partnership.
2. Dispose of the goodwill of the business.
3. Do any other act which would make it impossible to carry on the ordinary business of a partnership.
4. Confess a judgment.
5. Submit a partnership claim or liability to arbitration or reference.

If the partners cannot agree (are "deadlocked") on a fundamental matter and the business of the partnership is placed in irreparable jeopardy, a court may, at the request of a partner, order the partnership dissolved. This potential "veto power" which every partner may have under state law could be detrimental to the partnership. A partnership agreement can alter such rules which may otherwise be applicable to the management of the partnership in order to allocate management duties in virtually any manner which can be agreed upon by the partners.

☞ *STRATEGIC TIP*

The founder of a family business may find it useful to retain control of the business by having his children and other relatives sign a partnership agreement which empowers him, as managing partner, with sole authority for certain important decisions. Such an agreement may help ensure that an unhappy child or grandchild with a small partnership interest is not able to block the partnership from pursuing an advantageous opportunity or bind the partnership to an ill-advised arrangement.

Admission and Expulsion of Partners

A partnership agreement should set forth procedures for admitting new persons as partners and allowing existing partners to withdraw from the partnership. Under the laws of many states, a dissolution of the partnership could result when an existing general partner withdraws from the partnership. Accordingly, it may be appropriate for a partnership agreement to provide for the continuation of the partnership notwithstanding the withdrawal of a partner.

In developing procedures for admitting new partners and removing existing partners, you should consider what the consequences would be in the absence of such provisions. For example, it may be appropriate to include a provision in the partnership agreement authorizing a majority of the partners to expel another partner and restrict such expelled partner's rights in the assets of the partnership. It would, of course, be appropriate to condition exercise of the expulsion right on the commission of misconduct or a failure by a partner to perform his responsibilities diligently.

☞ *STRATEGIC TIP*

Partners in a family partnership may wish to agree on whether related family members should be freely admissible into the partnership or, if not, what limitations should apply. For example, two sisters may establish a successful partnership but, although they enjoy working with each other, they would not be interested in working with their respective brothers-in-law. A written partnership agreement can help set the parameters for permissible entry and departure into and out of the partnership.

Capital Contributions to the Partnership

Partners may contribute capital to the partnership in the form of cash or property which can be used to help finance partnership operations. In addition, and in the absence of state law impediments, some partners may contribute their time (services) as part or even all of their capital contribution. A capital contribution does not bear interest and is generally repayable only upon dissolution of the partnership. Over the course of time, it may be desirable or necessary for the partnership to seek additional capital contributions from its partners in order to remain in business or expand. It is usually desirable for the partners to agree on circumstances when each of them can be required to make additional contributions to the partnership and the consequences of a failure to abide by the agreement. A partnership agreement can be used to identify those circumstances which may require each partner to contribute (or loan) additional money to the partnership—and the consequences of a failure to do so.

☞ *STRATEGIC TIP*

A failure by a partner to advance additional funds to the partnership (whether by way of an additional capital contribution or loan) in accordance with his agreement could lead to a dilution or reduction of his interest in the partnership or a lawsuit for breach of contract. The more specifically the remedies for failing to contribute additional capital to the partnership are set forth in the written agreement, the easier it will be for partners to intelligently decide whether or not to make their respective contributions.

Allocation of Partnership Profits and Losses

In the absence of an agreement to the contrary, the laws of many states provide that a partnership's profits and/or losses are shared equally by the partners. Because "equal" is not always "equitable," it is commonplace for partners to agree on a different method for allocating profits and, perhaps, an even different method for allocating losses. The following provision under the

Delaware partnership law is an example of a typical form of statutory provision many states have enacted to reflect the ability of partners to "tailor" their relationships to each other:

> *The rights and duties of the partners in relation to the partnership shall be determined,* subject to any agreement between them, *by the following rules: (1) Each partner shall be repaid his contributions, whether by way of capital or advances to the partnership property, and share equally in the profits and surplus remaining after all liabilities, including those to partners, are satisfied; and must contribute toward the losses, whether of capital or otherwise, sustained by the partnership according to his share in the profits (emphasis added).*

☞ *STRATEGIC TIP*

The founder of a family partnership may find it desirable for estate planning purposes to give his children interests in the partnership without intending to give them the right to share in partnership profits equally. By agreeing on an appropriate allocation of profits and/or losses (which can be periodically revised), many objectives can be accomplished without wreaking financial injustice on those partners deserving a bigger share of profits.

Death of a Partner

Depending on the circumstances, it may be appropriate to include provisions dealing with the death of a partner. Under the laws of most states, absent an agreement among the partners to the contrary, the death of even a single general partner in a general partnership automatically results in a dissolution of the partnership. Moreover, a deceased partner's heirs can often force a sale of the partnership business and require the sale proceeds to be distributed to the partners in accordance with their respective interests. As a result, it is ordinarily advisable to provide in a partnership agreement that the business of the partnership is to be continued notwithstanding the occurrence of an event that would otherwise entail a dissolution.

☞ *STRATEGIC TIP*

Partnership agreements can also be useful for specifying the consequences of other "unusual" developments which may affect the partnership, such as the temporary or permanent disability of a partner, leaves of absences, etc. You may wish to consider how to address in an agreement circumstances or developments peculiar to your partnership which you reasonably expect to occur in order that such matters are handled smoothly.

The "Purpose" of the Partnership

Depending on how the management of the partnership is structured, it may be useful to include a provision in your partnership agreement setting forth the scope of contemplated partnership activities. For example, if the management of the partnership has been delegated to one partner (who is expected to be active in the business), other partners (who may be silent investors) may want to limit the managing partner's authority to act in furtherance of only those purposes agreed to by all the partners, as set forth in the partnership agreement.

Competition Among Partners

The "fiduciary duty" of trust and loyalty that partners owe one another is ordinarily broad enough to prohibit partners from competing with the partnership. This prohibition ordinarily requires business opportunities of interest to the partnership, which come to an individual partner's attention, to be offered to the partnership. For some partnerships, some or all of the partners may wish to retain their freedom to pursue other opportunities outside of the partnership, including opportunities which could be construed to be in competition with activities of the partnership. Accordingly, you should consider whether your partnership agreement should prohibit or permit such competition.

SHAREHOLDERS' AGREEMENTS

As previously discussed, corporations differ from other forms of business by having a management system that allocates certain rights and responsibilities to shareholders, directors and managers. Although the shareholders may have chosen to incorporate for a variety of reasons (such as the opportunity to limit their personal liability), they may prefer to "manage" the corporation as if they were partners. This preference may be based on a number of factors, including a desire by minority shareholders (i.e., shareholders with less than a 50 percent interest in the corporation) to ensure that they maintain some degree of control over corporate affairs and are not at risk of being automatically out-voted on every issue by the majority shareholders. A properly fashioned agreement among the shareholders — a "shareholders' agreement" — can often satisfy the objectives of all the shareholders. Shareholders' agreements are often useful for another important purpose as well. As a rule, stock of a corporation can be given or sold to any person or business, subject to compliance with applicable securities law. Accordingly, any family member or other person who acquires an ownership interest in a family business is free to give away or sell that ownership interest. Such free transferability may create a problem for the other family members in the business because the new owner may not share the same business goals as the family or, worse, may not trust or even like the family members and may seek to make life "difficult."

In order to eliminate this potential problem of dealing with nonfamily members, and to ensure that control and ownership of a family business remains lodged with family members, shareholders of a family-owned corporation frequently enter into a shareholders' agreement.

In addition to (1) establishing a mechanism for managing the corporation and (2) restricting the transferability of the corporation's stock, shareholders' agreements may address virtually any issue of importance to shareholders of a corporation, from issues of significant importance to issues most people may consider trivial. For example, the shareholders of a Subchapter S corporation may find it desirable to agree that they will not take any action which could jeopardize the corporation's Subchapter S status (such as the simple act of selling shares to a corporation — which cannot qualify as a Subchapter S shareholder). Shareholders may also find it desirable to restrict the transferability of shares to save the time and expense of registering the shares as securities under the federal securities law. Less important issues, such as which shareholder gets which office suite, can also be included in a shareholders' agreement. In short, shareholders' agreements can, and should, be tailored to address the unique concerns of the shareholders of a particular business. The following discussion is intended to suggest only some of the many items that may usefully be covered in your shareholders' agreement.

☞ *STRATEGIC TIP*

Although oral shareholders' agreements may be valid, it is usually desirable to put your agreement in writing. In the event of a dispute, the written document often proves more reliable than the shareholders' memories and courts are generally more willing to enforce a written shareholders' agreement than an oral agreement. Also, every new shareholder should be required to sign the shareholders' agreement to ensure that all shareholders are bound by its terms and conditions. It is possible, for example, for a shareholder to gift shares of stock in a family business to a child or grandchild who can cause irreparable damage to the business unless made a party to the agreement.

Maintaining Family Ownership

The following example may help clarify why many family members view shareholders' agreements as important to their business. Assume that Owl Bookstore, Inc. was founded by three brothers who each initially owned one-third of the stock of Owl. Each brother has since retired from the business and has transferred his stock in Owl to his sons and/or daughters. As a result, Owl is now owned by six shareholders. These six shareholders have varying interests in Owl: three desire to work at Owl full time, while the other three simply view their ownership in Owl as an investment. On the one hand, the three shareholders who are actively involved in managing Owl may be quite content to have their three inactive relatives own a percentage of Owl, but they would, on the other hand, vigorously object to a sale by such inactive family members to persons outside the family circle. The active shareholders may fear that any (new) nonfamily owners would be disruptive to Owl's operations. Accordingly, the active owners may seek to negotiate a shareholders' agreement with the inactive family members which prevents the inactive members from transferring Owl shares to nonfamily members.

Protecting "Outsiders" From Oppression

An outsider (i.e., a nonfamily member) who owns stock in a family business may have other reasons for entering into a shareholders' agreement. These reasons often reflect the fact that, because a corporation is managed by its board of directors, a shareholder will have little, if any, control over management unless he serves on (or can influence the composition of) the board of directors. A shareholder who is dissatisfied with a corporation's activities or performance can, of course, sell his shares *if* a buyer can be found. Unlike a shareholder of a public corporation whose shares are easily sold, an outside shareholder of a family-owned corporation may be unable to sell his shares if he becomes dissatisfied with his investment. Because a market for the shares of family-controlled corporations may be small or nonexistent, finding a buyer may be difficult or impossible.

The following example illustrates one of the risks of being a minority shareholder in a family-controlled business. Assume that Owl Bookstore, Inc. has six shareholders. Four of the shareholders collectively own 80 percent of Owl's stock. These four shareholders are all related to one another and are all employed (at generous salaries) by Owl. The other two shareholders (who collectively own 20 percent of Owl) are not family members (i.e., are "outside" investors) and are not employed by Owl. They made their investment in the hope of receiving annual dividends and that the value of their shares in Owl would increase. Over the past five years, however, Owl, acting through the board of directors elected by its four majority shareholder — employees, has increased their already-generous salaries. As a result of this increase, Owl's earnings, that might otherwise have been available to pay dividends to shareholders or to reinvest in Owl (thereby benefitting all shareholders alike), have benefitted only the majority owners. The outside minority shareholders have sought to sell their shares, but the only prospective purchaser backed away when he discovered that the current board of directors was channelling substantially all of Owl's earnings toward excessive salaries for the majority shareholder-employees.

In a situation like this, the minority shareholders will be powerless to oust the incumbent board of directors. Moreover, the minority shareholders will continue to have difficulty selling their shares because any potential new investor will see that the majority shareholders intend to use their control position to divert benefits from the shareholders, as a group, to themselves, in their capacity as employees. By entering into an appropriate shareholders' agreement (which, for example, may limit officers' compensation to a fixed amount), the minority shareholders may be able to restrict the extent to which the majority shareholders are able to take self-serving actions, such as salary increases.

Alternative Legal Solutions

Although we recommend that shareholders enter into an appropriate shareholders' agreement with one another to address a variety of issues (see below), we would be remiss if we failed to note that alternatives — albeit, we believe, less satisfactory — may exist to address some or all of these issues. For example, under general principles of corporate law, a board of directors owes a fiduciary duty of loyalty to the company's shareholders. The board violates this duty if it misappropriates benefits each shareholder should enjoy in proportion to his share ownership. Establishing a breach of fiduciary duty by the board of directors may, however, be difficult. In the example noted above, the board could argue that the high salaries it has authorized the corporation to pay to board members, in their capacity as employees, is justified by the quality and extent of their services to Owl. Moreover, bringing such a lawsuit will be time-consuming and the expense may far outweigh any benefit the minority shareholders would realize in the (by no means certain) event that they prevail.

☞ STRATEGIC TIP

In order to ensure that all shareholders have (1) some influence in the management of a corporation and (2) an opportunity and means for selling their shares in a corporation, we believe that the shareholders in a family-controlled corporation, whose shares are not publicly traded, should consider entering into an acceptable shareholders' agreement with one another.

Common Subjects of Shareholders' Agreements

A shareholders' agreement can reflect any term(s) the shareholders wish to impose on themselves and the corporation, except those terms that violate public policy. For example, a court would not enforce a restriction limiting a shareholder's ability to transfer his stock to members of only one sex, certain races, or certain religious persuasion. Depending on the shareholder's interests and bargaining power, terms may be negotiated to extend for virtually any period of time. Some subjects commonly included in a shareholders' agreement are:

Management. In order to ensure representation on a corporation's board of directors, an investor (or family member) can seek a contractual right to select a specified number of directors. The investor may also want to ensure that such a right to select a specified number of directors remains meaningful by restricting the corporation's ability to increase the size of the board. Absent such a restriction, the investor's contractual right could be rendered meaningless. For example, the right to select one of three directors may be "meaningful." If, however, the number of directorships is increased to ten, the right to select only one of the directors may be rendered virtually meaningless.

Shareholders in family corporations may wish to consider including a provision in their agreement which permits them to designate at least one or more directors in order to help ensure some representation on the board of directors. The shareholders' agreement can also be used to specify the process by which directors are to be selected.

Each board member, including those selected by minority investors, owes a fiduciary duty to all shareholders, not simply to the shareholder responsible for his selection to the board. Accordingly, although a director can be sensitive and responsive to the concerns and desires of the shareholder who designates him, he is not free to ignore his fiduciary obligation to act in the best interests of the corporation and the shareholders in general. Although it may be difficult to enforce as a practical matter, directors selected by one family faction must act in the best interest of all shareholders, including shareholders who may belong to a different family faction.

☞ STRATEGIC TIP

Shareholders' agreements can provide that the shareholders are to retain the authority to make decisions on certain issues typically left to the directors, such as, for example, the salary of all company officers.

Negative Covenants. Even if the shareholder has selected a "responsive" director, the director, as indicated above, owes a fiduciary duty to all shareholders and so may not always be in a position to accommodate the desire of the investor. Accordingly, an investor will often seek to include certain provisions known as "negative covenants" in a shareholders' agreement which prohibit the corporation from taking certain action without his consent. Examples of typical negative covenants include restrictions on the corporation's ability to: (1) pay dividends; (2) pay salaries to key employees in excess of specified levels; (3) borrow or spend money in excess of a certain amount without prior agreement; (4) sell a substantial part of its assets; (5) enter into a new line of business; and (6) engage in transactions with affiliates of the corporation. An investor who has obtained the benefit of such negative covenants can enforce such negative covenants whether or not they are in the best interest of the corporation or the other shareholders.

Preemptive Rights. An investor may desire to ensure that his percentage ownership interest in a corporation is not "diluted" should the corporation decide to issue additional stock to existing or additional investors. The investor's desire to protect his percentage interest can be satisfied if the investor obtains a contractual right to purchase a sufficient percentage of the new shares which the corporation plans to issue. Such a right is known as a "preemptive right." Preemptive rights take a number of forms, but, essentially, seek to protect existing investors from having their percentage of ownership in a corporation diluted through additional issuances of stock by the corporation.

Transferability Restrictions. A wide variety of restrictions on the transferability of a corporation's shares may be included in shareholders' agreements, reflecting a variety of shareholders' objectives. These restrictions often have confusing names but are typically straightforward in operation. The following discussion identifies the most common forms of transferability restrictions.

1. Right of First Refusal. A right of first refusal restricts a shareholder's ability to transfer his shares of stock to a third party without first offering them to the corporation and/or to the other existing shareholders. The corporation and/or other shareholders are given the right to purchase the shares at the same price as the sale price agreed to by the third party and the selling shareholder. If the corporation and/or the shareholders decline to exercise their "right of first refusal," the selling shareholder is free to sell his shares to the third party.

☞ *STRATEGIC TIP*

Shareholders often agree to give one another a right of first refusal to each other's shares to limit and/or control who becomes a shareholder of the corporation. For example, if an aging shareholder of a family-owned business wants to sell his interest in the business, the other family members/shareholders may want an opportunity to buy his shares so that a nonfamily member does not acquire an interest in their business.

2. Bring-Along Right. A bring-along right requires a minority shareholder to sell his shares of a corporation's stock to a third party whose offer to acquire 100 percent of the corporation's stock has been accepted by a majority of the shareholders.

A controlling shareholder of a corporation may want to preserve his ability to sell the entire corporation if a third party makes an attractive offer for the business. This may particularly be the case if the controlling shareholder has given up shares to nonfamily member employees as part of an incentive compensation package. Absent a "bring-along right," the controlling shareholder may be unable to force the minority shareholder to sell his shares to the third party. The inability of the controlling shareholder to ensure a sale of all outstanding shares could preclude a proposed acquisition if the third party is only interested in acquiring all of the outstanding stock of the corporation. As noted in chapter seven ("Selling [or Buying] Your Family Business"), a controlling shareholder may agree with the third-party offeror to transfer the entire corporation by way of a merger. A merger can generally be consummated by approval of a majority (or in some states two-thirds) vote of the outstanding shares. Even shareholders who oppose the merger and vote against it lose their ownership interest in the corporation upon completion of the merger, although, if they object to the consideration offered by the third party, they can exercise "dissenter's rights" pursuant to which a court will determine the amount that must be paid for their shares. If the third party prefers to structure the acquisition in another fashion, however, a "bring-along right" may become important.

3. Participation ("Tag Along") Right. Unlike a bring-along right, a participation (or "tag along") right gives a minority shareholder the right to sell his shares to a third party who has offered to acquire the shares of a controlling shareholder. The controlling shareholder will be unable to sell his shares unless he can convince the prospective buyer to acquire the shares of the minority shareholder as well.

☞ *STRATEGIC TIP*

A minority shareholder may wish to negotiate for a participation right if he would not want a new controlling shareholder to enter the business. He may want to ensure that he can exit the business at the same time and on the same terms as the controlling shareholder. The minority shareholder should be careful that the participation right included in the shareholders' agreement prohibits the controlling shareholder from selling his stock at an artificially low price and later reaping a windfall (at the expense of the minority shareholder) by obtaining an employment or consulting agreement with the purchaser following completion of the sale of the business.

4. Call and Put Rights. A "call" right entitles the owner (or "holder") of such a contractual right to buy the shares subject to the call at an agreed-upon price (or in accordance with an agreed-upon formula) within a specified time period.

A "put" right entitles the owner (or "holder") of such a contractual right to sell the shares subject to the put at an agreed-upon price (or in accordance with an agreed-upon formula) within a specified time period.

☞ *STRATEGIC TIP*

If the value of a company's stock increases, the value of the call right also increases (because the holder of the call can still purchase stock subject to the call at the agreed-upon price). If the value of stock declines, the value of a put right increases (because the holder of the put will still be able to sell the stock subject to the put at the agreed-upon price, regardless of the decline in the market price).

Remedies for Breach

States recognize, through both statutes and case precedent, that shareholders' agreements are contractual agreements which can be enforced in the event one party breaches the agreement. Traditional "defenses" to enforcement of a contract—such as, for example, fraud, duress, etc.—may also be raised as defenses in an action to enforce a shareholders' agreement. Although the circumstances of each breach of agreement are different—and so the damages sustained by the nonbreaching party—courts generally seem more inclined to order "specific performance" of the agreement than to enter an order awarding monetary damages. The reason for this remedy (which requires the parties to perform their agreement) is that it is often difficult or impossible to measure the extent of monetary damages that the nonbreaching party has sustained. In the event that the parties to a shareholders' agreement dispute the interpretation to be given to their agreement in particular circumstances, it is usually possible to bring a so-called declaratory judgment action in court to have the court resolve the dispute and clarify the agreement's application.

☞ STRATEGIC TIP

Even if available, monetary damages may not provide you with satisfactory "relief" in the event a party to your shareholders' agreement disregards its terms. By including a provision in the agreement itself that the parties agree to specific performance of the agreement you may, in the event of breach, strengthen your position in court for obtaining such relief.

VOTING TRUST AGREEMENTS

In a voting trust agreement, shareholders of a corporation agree to deposit their shares of stock with one or more voting trustee(s), who, in turn, actually vote the shares on behalf of the shareholders. Among other things, by entering into a voting trust agreement, shareholders may ensure that the voting power of their respective shares will be combined and, as the following example illustrates, that their heirs will be treated fairly.

Assume that two brothers each own fifty percent of a manufacturing company. They have been the sole shareholders of the company since they founded it twenty years earlier. Each has a son that he wants to bring into the business in the hope that the son will succeed him as co-head of the business upon his retirement. For a variety of reasons, either shareholder does not want to be a partner with the other shareholder's son. The question then arises as to how to structure an arrangement whereby each shareholder could, upon his retirement, transfer his fifty-percent ownership interest in the business to his son without thereby leaving the other shareholder (who has not yet retired) with an unwanted partner.

The solution to this dilemma may be to have the two shareholders enter into a voting trust agreement between themselves, in their capacity as voting trustees, and in their capacity as beneficial owners of the shares. As voting trustees, each would have an equal vote on all matters submitted to shareholders; as beneficial owners, each would be free to transfer all or a portion of his shares to his son without thereby giving up voting control over the shares and forcing an unwanted partner on the other co-owner. In the event that one of the voting trustees dies, voting control over the shares held in the voting trust could reside solely in the other voting trustee until he dies or retires and transfers his shares to his son. At such time when each son owns his father's shares, the voting trust agreement would terminate and each son would have direct control over his fifty-percent interest in the business.

The decision to use a voting trust agreement may simply be the first step towards solving the objectives of co-owners. Like so many situations, the solution to one problem raises other problems. In the case of the two co-owners discussed above, a potential problem with using a voting trust is that once one of the owners dies, the other acquires voting power over all of the outstanding shares (including those held by the son of the deceased shareholder). The surviving owner could use his voting power to benefit himself and his son at the expense of the deceased owner's son, whose shares continue to be subject to the voting trust. For example, the surviving owner may cause the corporation to enter into an employment agreement with his son which provides for a salary substantially in excess of the salary paid to his nephew. The surviving owner may also have the corporation provide a car, country club membership and other "perks" to his son without providing comparable benefits to his nephew. Accordingly, before you execute a voting trust agreement, you should consider agreeing with your co-owners upon certain contractual restrictions which may help ensure that your respective heirs will all be treated fairly during the period in which one of you (as surviving owner) holds sole voting control over the shares of the corporation.

☞ *STRATEGIC TIP*

Before creating and entering into a voting trust agreement, you should consider with your attorney its possible consequences. Such agreements may have adverse income tax consequences, they may trigger certain (expensive) registration requirements under the securities laws, etc. You will want to consider such possible consequences before entering into a voting trust agreement.

Remedies for Breach

As with shareholders' agreements, courts seem generally more willing to enforce a breach of a voting trust agreement by ordering the parties to perform their agreement in accordance with its terms (as opposed to awarding monetary damages, which may be difficult to measure and which may be an inadequate remedy). If you decide to enter into a voting trust agreement, you and your co-owners may wish to include a provision in the agreement which specifies what the remedies for breach of agreement should be, in some or all circumstances.

☞ STRATEGIC TIP

The foregoing example underscores a typical pattern: a businessman will have a goal that he wants to achieve, and achievement of the goal requires a creative solution. However, implementation of the solution presents other problems or leaves the businessman exposed to a risk he might not otherwise have faced. Certain problems and risks can be addressed with minimal time and expense if they are identified; others can be addressed only at great time and expense. Judgment must be exercised to determine whether the time and effort of dealing with the problem is warranted in light of the benefit that would be realized by addressing it.

MISCELLANEOUS AGREEMENTS

This chapter provides an overview on the nature and variety of agreements which co-owners of a business can reach to help them agree on objectives and avoid disputes. The subject matter for such agreements can include virtually any issue or facet of business operations and the mechanisms for implementing such agreements can be narrow or broad, depending on the interest of the parties involved. For example, co-owners of a business may agree: (1) to give each other a power to "veto" some or all corporate decisions; (2) to define the circumstances under which dividends will be paid (and when earnings will be reinvested in the business); and (3) to identify individuals who will serve as officers of their corporation, and the amount of their salary for such service.

States often have different rules relating to the enforceability of such agreements and you should, again, be careful to discuss with your attorney the subject of such agreements which may be of interest to you, and whether such agreements are lawful in your state.

Chapter Five

Disagreements Among Owners

E ach of us, in one way or another, has probably disagreed with our respective friends, colleagues or family members on a variety of issues, both big and small. Such is human nature. Family businesses are not immune from interpersonal disagreements or controversies among its participants. As with other disagreements, some may be productive and, ultimately, beneficial to the business; others may be counterproductive and destroy a family business and the family itself. This chapter explores the most common sources of disagreement among owners of a family business and then suggests a variety of preventative measures that may assist the owners in resolving their disagreements before the disagreements wreak personal and financial havoc on the family. Because of the complexity and importance of the issues raised in this chapter, you will want to consult your attorney in predispute planning discussions as well as when actually faced with a dispute with your co-owner(s).

THE UNIQUE NATURE OF DISAGREEMENT IN A FAMILY BUSINESS

When owners in a family business disagree on virtually any aspect of the business, the personal and financial stakes are usually different from those stakes in other disagreements. First, generations of blood, sweat and tears may be placed at risk by a disagreement which threatens the business' continuing viability. Along with this risk comes the risk that family members who have come to rely on the job security provided by the business — and who are otherwise unsuited or untrained for other employment — may be displaced from their jobs.

Second, unlike businesses whose stock is widely or publicly

traded, stock in a family business may be difficult or impossible to sell to a third party, either because of an applicable restrictive stock agreement or because an outsider may not be interested in a minority position in a family business. The difficulties associated with disposing of stock in a family business may be exacerbated if, as is often the case, such stock represents a large part of the owner's personal wealth.

Third, disagreements among family members which are not resolved can build to a boiling point, resulting in bitter relationships where the unhappy owner's aim is to obstruct and hinder business operations rather than improve them. It is not unheard of for such disagreements to lead to family strife, intrafamily litigation and, indeed, physical violence. Disputes that might lead nonfamily members simply to quit their job or sell their ownership interest may, in the case of family members, generate personal animosity and unproductive behavior yet, because of their status in the family, make them more reluctant to leave their business.

SOURCES OF DISPUTES

Perhaps the most important prerequisite to resolving disputes is to first recognize that potentially explosive disputes can be caused by a virtually unlimited number of events. Co-owners of a family business may come to dislike or distrust each other over time. They may lose professional respect for each other as business owners and managers. Their children may dislike or be jealous of each other. They may disagree on business philosophy—whether to pursue new business ventures or stay with the tried and true business that produced, perhaps, great wealth for the family. Some owners may even feel cheated or defrauded by their co-owners (which feelings are sometimes justified and sometimes not). Co-owners may disagree on compensation, hiring and firing of family members, or whether the business should be sold or dissolved. They may have brought an outsider into the business who sides with one faction of the family and, in so doing, adds fuel to the fire of bitterness. In short, the root causes of intrafamily disputes result from many different factors for many different reasons. Recognizing that all such disputes are potentially devastating to the business and the family members, one or more suitable mechanisms should be considered so that when a dispute arises—in any form — the family and business can resolve it effectively and with the least possible trauma.

Although there are a virtually unlimited number of sources out of which a dispute may arise, it is our experience that four particular issues seem to cause an undue proportion of intrafamily problems. These issues are:

1. Disagreements as to appropriate business strategy. For example, should the business expand into a new product line or make an acquisition; should the business increase its advertising budget or make additional capital expenditures; should the business hire additional personnel? Such disagreements are not unique to family businesses.

2. Disagreements as to the relative skills and talents of family members and their relative entitlements to compensation, responsibility, advancement opportunities, etc. In many family businesses, employees may rise within the business, not by virtue of their skills and talents, but by virtue of their status as family members. Such preferential treatment may, on the one hand, be the essence of a family business and yet may also be the catalyst for a business' failure to achieve enduring success. At some point, leaders of the family business must make a choice between promoting the interests of the business (and hence promoting the persons best able to further the interests of the business) or promoting family members who may not be as capable as other available personnel. A failure to agree on this choice often spells destruction for a family business.

3. Lack of open and honest communication. Whereas open and honest communication in the context of a nonfamily business may not entail emotional repercussions, such communication can severly strain family business relations and result in a lack of open and honest communication. For example, if a leader of the family business criticizes the performance of his nephew, the mother of the nephew (i.e., the sister of the leader of the family business) may end up refusing to talk to her brother.

4. A failure to respect each family member's contribution to the business. In "extended" family businesses, for example, some cousins may feel that their own contributions are invaluable while those of their relatives are useless. These feelings are difficult to hide and can cause problems. If appropriate effort is not made to

focus on both the good and bad of each family member's contributions, paralyzing dissension can envelop a family business.

Hopefully, you and your business' co-owners can resolve your disputes through open and amicable discussions. In the event you cannot, the mechanisms discussed in the balance of this chapter may prove to be particularly important to your business.

MECHANISMS FOR RESOLVING DISPUTES

There are basically two paths that co-owners can follow to resolve their disputes. First, they can agree on a mechanism or procedure to resolve their dispute in one fashion or another. Such agreements may be made at any time—prior to commencement of business operations through to the time when an actual dispute exists. It is ordinarily preferable if the co-owners can agree ahead of time on the mechanism they will use to resolve their disputes, because there is usually more rationality and less emotion involved in the parties' choice of dispute resolution procedure as a result. Also, if they cannot agree on such a procedure in advance of an actual dispute, it is doubtful that they will be able to agree on a procedure if they have an actual dispute.

In the event that co-owners of a business are unable to reach a voluntary resolution of their dispute (or agree on a mechanism for resolving their disputes), all states have provisions in their business law which may "force" a resolution upon the co-owners. Such involuntary resolutions can require the forced sale or dissolution of a business. The following sections provide an overview of both voluntary and involuntary dispute resolution mechanisms that may be available to resolve paralyzing disputes among co-owners.

VOLUNTARY RESOLUTIONS

Arbitration

One of the most common methods used in resolving family business disagreements is for the family members (and other co-owners, if any) to agree to submit their dispute to one or more disinterested individuals who are vested with the authority to suggest or impose a solution to the dispute. These disinterested individuals are commonly referred to as "arbitrators."

Advantages. There are a number of advantages to the arbitration process. First, a successful family business is ordinarily something to be treasured and preserved — not something that should be sold in the event of a disagreement or deadlock among co-owners. Many unhappy owners may, in any event, find it difficult or impossible to sell their partial (minority) interests in a business. Second, arbitration (unlike litigation in court) can be kept relatively confidential; it is also generally faster and cheaper than resolving a dispute in court. Third, co-owners can give arbitrators broad authority to fashion an appropriate remedy. Judges may, however, find it difficult or impossible to fashion similar remedies because they are limited by applicable judicial or legislative constraints. Finally, if the parties to a dispute recognize that they cannot "force" a deadlock and that their positions (which they know may be unreasonable) will be submitted for arbitration, they may find it easier to resolve their own disputes consensually.

Disadvantages. There may also be disadvantages associated with the arbitration process which you should consider. First, arbitrators, no matter how smart or experienced, may simply be inappropriate people to make major policy decisions for a family business. Whether your family expands into a new line of operations at a cost of thousands (or millions) of dollars is, for example, a decision that perhaps should only be made by the family members whose money is to be invested. Second, it may be difficult to draft an agreement which clearly defines those disputes which should be submitted for arbitration and those which should not. Presumably, every minor grievance should not become arbitrable. Finally, many businessmen and professional counselors believe that it will be impossible for business partners to cooperate with each other in the long run if they are unable to resolve their own disagreements. Accordingly, any mechanism that hinders co-owners from resolving their own disputes among themselves may ultimately prove detrimental to the long-term health of the family business.

In the event you believe the advantages of arbitration outweigh its disadvantages, you should carefully consider (with your professional advisors) how the law in your state may shape the permissible scope of your arbitration agreement. Some states are more receptive than others in allowing co-owners of a business to resolve their disputes through arbitration. Indeed, in certain states, there may be some types of disputes that cannot be resolved through arbitration but can only be addressed by litigation.

☞ *STRATEGIC TIP*

The parties to an arbitration agreement should also consider identifying the individual (or institution) who will serve as arbitrator in the event of a dispute or, alternatively, inserting a provision addressing how the arbitrator(s) are to be selected in the event a dispute arises. The failure to select from a variety of options may permit one party to a business dispute to hinder the arbitration process by failing to agree on the selection of an arbitrator.

Outside Consultant

An alternative to arbitration is for the family business to engage an outside consultant. Presumably, the outside consultant will be a person whose experience and qualifications will command the respect of the warring factions of the family. By virtue of this person's qualifications, he will, perhaps, be in a position to provide advice which the family members respect. Frequently, advice from an outsider will be respected and accepted even if the same advice from the mouth of another family member would be dismissed as self-serving or antagonistic.

☞ *STRATEGIC TIP*

Perhaps one advantage of using an outside consultant is that a consultant traditionally makes only nonbinding observations and recommendations to the family members. The nonbinding nature of the consultant's role may make it easier for many family members to consider this dispute resolution mechanism because there is no perceived loss of control by the owners. If a member or the entire family dislikes the consultant's recommendations, they are not necessarily bound by them.

Settlement Agreements

As with other types of disputes, co-owners of a business may reach a formal settlement of their dispute which, when put in writing, may help the co-owners to coexist more peacefully in the future. Such agreements may address virtually any subject of dispute, ranging from the identity of officers and directors (and their salaries) to perhaps more minor issues, such as the amount of vacation time that family members who are active in the business may take.

The scope of such "settlement agreements" is virtually unlimited and may be as wide as those issues which are the subject of a "shareholders' agreement." In effect, business co-owners have at least two opportunities to limit or resolve their disputes by contract: first, in anticipation of potential future disputes, in a shareholders' agreement, and second, in response to a present, actual dispute, in a settlement agreement. It is usually more advantageous and less disruptive for everyone if an agreement can be reached beforehand on certain issues as it may permit parties to guide their conduct by an acceptable, agreed-upon standard.

Business Spin-Offs

Another alternative to resolving a family business dispute that may be worth considering is for the family co-owners to divide their single business into two or more component parts. The disputing family factions could take over their own component parts of the business, which could either be run as a "division" of the existing business (with profits divided in proportion to the relative profitability of the divisions) or as entirely new businesses (with no such profit sharing).

If the "spin-off" alternative is pursued, each disputing faction should consider not just the strengths and weaknesses of each potential new division (or separate new business) but how such changes can be accomplished with minimum tax liability and minimum disruption to the ongoing operations of the business. You should consult your advisors about the possibility of accomplishing your objectives through tax-free spin-offs and exchanges.

Buy-Out of Dissenting Shareholder

In addition to the use of a buy-out agreement for other reasons, a buy-out agreement can also be used to resolve disputes among co-owners. Generally, co-owners are free to agree that, in the event they develop an irreconcilable difference of opinions, one co-owner can buy the interest of the other co-owner(s) in the business.

Buy-out agreements, which usually make sense only after other attempts to resolve the dispute have failed, can be structured so as to give one or all of the co-owners the opportunity to buy out the other co-owners. One advantage to this solution is that it preserves the family business for at least some family members while the other members may receive a fair price in exchange for their interest. The parties, of course, will need to decide in advance what the price will be — or what formula should be used to determine the price.

☞ *STRATEGIC TIP*

Perhaps one disadvantage with the buy-out option is that it may give one group (such as the majority owners) an incentive to precipitate a dispute in order to force out their co-owners, who may otherwise have preferred to remain in the business. Therefore, it is important to carefully draft your agreement to reduce or eliminate this possibility.

One approach to dealing with such a possibility is to provide that any shareholder may offer to buy out the interests of the other shareholders at a specified price per share. The other shareholders would then be free to either accept the buy-out offer or to purchase the offering shareholder's shares at the price he offered. This right to make a "counter-offer," presumably discourages bad faith and unfair initial offers. For example, assume that there are five shareholders of Owl Bookstores, and each shareholder owns twenty shares of stock in Owl. If a dispute arises among the shareholders, one shareholder, John Smith, may make a buy-out offer to each of the other four shareholders. Smith may offer to buy out the interests of each of the other shareholders at the price of $1 per share. The other shareholders would then have the opportunity to accept Smith's buy-out offer or, alternatively, buy out Smith's interest in the business for a price of $1 per share. In this scenario, Smith would presumably only offer to buy out the other shareholders at $1 per share if he believes the buy-out offer is fair, and he would be willing to sell his own shares on such terms because he risks being forced to sell his shares at a price equal to the price he proposed paying to the other shareholders.

Sale of the Business

Perhaps the final solution to resolving a business dispute is for the co-owners to agree to sell the entire business to an unrelated third party. This agreement could be made at any time, before the start of operations in anticipation of a substantial dispute up until the time a substantial dispute actually exists. On the one hand, a planned solution to sell a business if a substantial dispute ever arises has some semblance of fairness: each co-owner is treated equally because the "other side" didn't get their way in resolving the business dispute and the terms of the sale are the same for everyone. On the other hand, some family members who have worked longer and harder hours than other family members may feel they are being unfairly forced out of business. Sometimes, these family members may feel disinclined to work longer and harder for the good of the business because of the threat of a forced sale of the business. This "disincentive" may, of course, have a self-fulfilling aspect to it (why work longer or harder in the first place if the business will be sold anyway?).

☞ *STRATEGIC TIP*

Sometimes, providing an appropriate mechanism to permit an owner to buy out his co-owners can solve this problem. The mechanism, to be fair, should give each co-owner the same opportunity to buy out the other co-owner's business interest. If each owner is interested in remaining in the business, an alternative solution may be found.

Miscellaneous

Because of the flexibility a corporation affords for doing business, there are, perhaps, unlimited variations of the foregoing strategies for seeking a voluntary resolution of disputes among shareholders. By manipulating the characteristics of stock (e.g., voting, nonvoting, redeemable); directorships (e.g., electability, numbers of, period of tenure); etc., co-owners can continually refine their relationship with each other. Similar opportunities exist, to varying degrees, with other business forms, including general and limited partnerships. You may wish to consider with your attorney possible alternative dispute resolution mechanisms.

INVOLUNTARY RESOLUTIONS

In the event that co-owners of a business are unable to resolve their disputes voluntarily, they may, depending on the state law to which the business and its owners are subject, have a number of options, which, if exercised, could impose an involuntary resolution on the parties to a dispute. We do note, of course, that one "option" is for the co-owners to simply live with their differences. There are, unfortunately, many family businesses where the co-owners literally hate working with each other but, for a variety of reasons (usually economic), they prefer to maintain the status quo rather than sell the business or their interest in it. These situations typically continue to deteriorate until conditions are so bad that another solution must be found. The following section summarizes some of the most common of such solutions.

Voluntary Dissolution

Every state offers shareholders a mechanism by which they can voluntarily dissolve their corporation. Some states require that the board of directors propose the corporation's dissolution to its shareholders, who then decide the issue, typically either by simple majority in interest vote or two-thirds in interest vote. Some states permit shareholders to raise the issue of voluntary dissolution on their own.

☞ STRATEGIC TIP

Because *majority* shareholders are ordinarily able to cause a voluntary dissolution of their corporations by voting only their shares, there have been instances where *minority* shareholders have been unfairly forced out of business. In recognition of this problem, many states now provide that majority owners cannot "squeeze-out" minority shareholders by offering or causing them to receive less than fair compensation for their shares. Such conduct may constitute a breach of the majority owner's fiduciary duty to the minority owner, which could make him liable to the minority owner for monetary damages in a court of law. Accordingly, any co-owner proposing or responding to this option should exercise great caution and discuss his plans with his attorneys.

Court-Ordered Dissolution

Every state provides that corporations can be dissolved by court order for a variety of reasons. Although these reasons vary from state to state, the most common reasons include the following:

Shareholder Deadlock. Most states provide that a corporation can be ordered dissolved in the event that the directors are deadlocked and the shareholders are unable to break the deadlock and, as a result of the deadlock, the corporation will suffer irreparable injury. For example, the Pennsylvania Business Corporation Law provides that "upon application filed by a shareholder or director of a business corporation, the court may entertain proceedings for the involuntary winding up and dissolution of the corporation when any of the following is made to appear: . . . (3) the directors are deadlocked in the direction of the management of the business and affairs of the corporation and the shareholders are unable to break the deadlock and that irreparable injury to the corporation is being suffered or is threatened by reason thereof. The court shall not appoint a receiver or grant other similar relief under this paragraph if the shareholders by agreement or otherwise have provided for the appointment of a provisional director or other means for the resolution of a deadlock but the court shall enforce the remedies so provided if appropriate."

☞ STRATEGIC TIP

Many state courts have historically shown a reluctance to dissolve a profitable corporation simply because of a shareholder deadlock. In recognizing the discretionary (as opposed to mandatory) nature of this remedy, courts have occasionally suggested that the shareholders' "best interests" would not be served by a court-ordered dissolution of their business. Under this traditional standard, unless the business itself were jeopardized, shareholder deadlock would not always result in dissolution of the business. Today, many courts seem more willing to dissolve a corporation when shareholder deadlock is accompanied by hostility and bitterness, regardless of whether a dissolution may not otherwise be in the shareholders' "best interest." If appropriate, you should discuss the applicable legal standard for this solution in your state with your attorney.

Shareholder Misconduct. Most states also permit shareholders to seek a court order dissolving a corporation in the event that the "controlling shareholders" have acted illegally or unfairly with respect to the other shareholders. Such conduct may include fraud on the minority shareholders, theft or waste of corporate assets, or other acts which are unfair or "oppressive" to the minority shareholders. For example, the Pennsylvania Business Corporation Law authorizes the Court to entertain proceedings for the involuntary winding up and dissolution of the corporation when "(1) the acts of the directors, or those in control of the corporation, are illegal, oppressive or fraudulent and . . . it is beneficial to the interests of the shareholders that the corporation be wound up and dissolved" or "the corporate assets are being misapplied or wasted and . . . it is beneficial to the interests of the shareholders that the corporation be wound up and dissolved."

Judicial standards for oppressive conduct sufficient to justify dissolution vary from state to state and are constantly changing. Many courts appear to focus their attention on whether the parties' conduct was, under all the circumstances, unfair. One way the owners of a business can help reduce the likelihood of a dispute on the definition of unfair conduct is for them to agree, before commencing business, on the scope of their relationship and their expectations of each other. This agreement (which could be made part of a shareholders' agreement) could be useful for the owners and the court for determining what is (or is not) fair.

Buy-Out in Lieu of Dissolution

A number of states now provide that shareholders can force (as opposed to agree upon) a buy-out of their co-owners in certain limited situations. Although these situations vary from state to state, many courts may permit a buy-out (typically by the majority of the minority owners' interest) if, under all the circumstances, it is a fair and reasonable alternative to dissolution.

☞ *STRATEGIC TIP*

In the event a buy-out is ordered by a court, the buy-out price must be determined. The parties, in seeking to establish the value of the interest being bought or sold, should consider the applicability of discounting the price to reflect relevant factors, such as the lack of marketability of the shares, covenants not to compete which may be negotiated with the seller, etc. If a minority interest is being acquired, it is worth keeping in mind that a court may not allow a "minority discount" on the valuation of the minority interest where the purchaser is not an outside third party but, rather, the controlling shareholder.

Miscellaneous

In addition to the remedies noted above, which traditionally have been the most frequently used "involuntary" solutions to disputes among co-owners, courts have shown an increasing willingness to resolve such disputes by fashioning specific remedies which may be more appropriate to the particular facts and circumstances before it. For example, courts have been prepared to order shareholders to "cease and desist" from engaging in oppressive conduct; to rescind a corporate act that is oppressive or unfair to only certain shareholders; and to order financial compensation to shareholders who have been victimized by their co-owners. Courts may also appoint provisional directors, custodians and receivers to help run a business until a solution to a substantial dispute has been worked out. Perhaps the only limit on the scope of such remedies is the imagination of the court and of your attorney (although, of course, the constraints of judicial precedent and legislation cannot be ignored).

☞ STRATEGIC TIP

It is important to remember—no matter what side of a dispute you may be on—that courts may be increasingly willing to use their authority creatively and flexibly to fashion a fair remedy or solution to a dispute among co-owners. Accordingly, in working with your co-owners, you should strive to be fair—not only because it is appropriate and "the right thing to do," but because you may be forced to be fair in court!

Chapter Six

Compensating Owners, Directors and Employees

B ecause a family business, like virtually every kind of business, is operated with the goal of making a profit, compensation issues take on priority importance to the owners and employees of the business. If compensation decisions are made in a manner that owners and employees perceive to be fair and equitable, relations among the owners and employees tend to be harmonious. If owners and employees perceive their respective compensation levels as disproportionately low in relation to their respective contributions to the business, relations generally sour and the operation of the business is likely to be impaired.

Generally, a business seeks to compensate persons who fall into one of three categories: (1) the shareholder-owners; (2) the board of directors; and (3) the employees. In many family businesses, family members are shareholders, directors *and* employees, and receive compensation for each of these positions.

Compensation may take many forms. For owners, compensation may refer to the "return on investment" when a business is sold. Legal aspects of selling a business are explored in more detail in the following chapter. Perhaps more typically, ownership compensation refers to dividend payments funded from the earnings of the business. For employees, compensation represents the current and deferred *monetary* return a person receives in exchange for his labor. However, as the phrase, "the work is its own reward" indicates, for many people, the compensation received from work need not be viewed simply in monetary terms. Intangibles, such as a large office, an impressive job title or simple job gratification, are all forms of compensation. Stated differently, people are not motivated solely by money. Although money is a great motivator, many people are motivated by other considerations. For example, if a business values an employee, but is unable or unwilling to pay him as much money as he would like, the business may be able to keep the employee happy and motivated by giving him a more exalted title. Jane Smith, for example, may feel better about herself (and hence be more highly motivated) if she is given the title of "Chief Administrative Supervisor" rather than simply known as head of secretaries. Similarly, Cynthia Smith may perform her job with greater confidence and, hence, more effectiveness if she is given the title of "Vice President" rather than a less prestigious or no title at all. In addition, many employees are willing to accept a reduced salary in exchange for job security.

In this chapter, we identify different approaches to compensating owners, directors and employees of the family business and various considerations that bear on these approaches. This chapter does not address the dynamics and strategies of negotiating the level or form of compensation, which, of course, is an art unto itself (and about which many good books have already been written). We simply note that such dynamics will vary greatly depending on a variety of factors, such as whether or not you are the sole owner of your business, whether you have children (and nieces and nephews) who are also employees, and whether your employees are members of a union.

COMPENSATING OWNERS

Owners of a business, in their capacity as shareholders or partners, receive compensation in the form of dividends (or distributions) on their stock or partnership interests, respectively. The dividends or distributions made to owners of the business will not be deductible to the business, but will be included in the income of the owners. Generally, the amount of dividends paid to the owners is determined by the board of directors (or other governing body) of the business entity. Once the board of directors has determined the amount of money available for distribution to the owners, the amount is distributed pro rata to the shareholder-owners in accordance with their ownership interests. State law generally restricts a corporation's ability to pay dividends in order to ensure that a corporation does not distribute excessive funds to shareholders and thereby leave the corporation with an insufficient amount of funds for satisfying liabilities of the business. You should consider these legal limitations with your attorney.

Dividends vs. Retention of Funds

A tension exists between providing owners of the business with a return on their investment in the form of dividends and retaining funds in the business to enable the business to grow. Senior members of the family are usually more concerned about maintaining their lifestyle (and so cash flow) while junior family members may be more interested in reinvesting earnings to help ensure business growth over the long haul. Sometimes this tension can be resolved by issuing preferred stock (that pays regular dividends) to senior owners and issuing common stock (that might not pay dividends but represents the residual ownership interest in the business with "growth potential") to junior owners. Striking an appropriate balance between dividends and retention of funds is a primary responsibility of the board of directors.

COMPENSATING DIRECTORS

Directors may be compensated in a variety of ways. Many corporations pay directors a fixed annual amount and reimburse them for travel expenses incurred in attending board meetings. It is not unusual for public corporations to grant directors stock options in order to give them an initiative to take action designed to promote the growth and profitability of the business. In many family businesses, however, granting such stock options to directors may less frequently occur because the owners do not want to dilute their sole (or family) ownership. Family members who serve on the board may receive additional compensation for their board service, depending on the particular policy of the family business.

COMPENSATING EMPLOYEES

Although there are many approaches that may be taken to compensate employees, the following are the most common:

Salary

The traditional approach to compensating employees is to provide them with a salary. Salaries are typically payable on a weekly, biweekly or monthly basis in exchange for services rendered. Generally, the more valuable an employee's contributions to a business, the higher his salary. An employee's salary will be taxable to the employee as ordinary income in the year received and is generally deductible by the business in the year paid.

It is not unusual for only some members of a family to work for their business. Other members may be interested in pursuing other endeavors or may be unable to work for their family business (say, for example, because they marry a spouse whose job is in another locality). By giving each family member stock in the business, some family planning objectives may be secured. The family-member employees receive salaries for their efforts as employees. In addition, *all* family members, as shareholders, may receive dividends to reflect their status as owners. In the event the business is sold, moreover, each family-member owner will receive a share of the sale proceeds equal to his or her ownership share. Care should be given to ensure that compensation of employees is fair so that an unduly large percentage of earnings is not siphoned off from potential distribution to the shareholders.

If the compensation paid to an employee-shareholder is unreasonably high, the Internal Revenue Service may challenge the ability of the business to deduct a portion of the salary. The IRS may claim that the excessively high salary is, in reality, a "disguised" (nondeductible) dividend. Accordingly, family-owned businesses must be careful to ensure that the salaries they pay to shareholder-employees are reasonable so that they can be deducted as reasonable compensation. One method to help measure the reasonableness of compensation is to compare the salaries paid to other employees, performing comparable work, for a nonfamily owned business in the same or related industry. Salary payments substantially in excess of this "industry standard" may be particularly susceptible to attack by the IRS.

Hourly Wages

Many workers are paid wages based on the number of hours they work. Unlike salaried employees, who receive a fixed annual amount, an hourly wage earner's pay is tied to the range of hours he works. The tax treatment of salary and wages is the same.

Bonuses

Bonuses take many forms, but can generally be characterized as either discretionary or nondiscretionary depending on the nature of the employer's commitment to pay the bonus. A bonus is often a valuable tool for giving workers an incentive to exert their best efforts on behalf of the business. In small businesses, a bonus frequently takes the form of a year-end "extraordinary payment" to valued workers. In larger businesses, key employees more typically negotiate employment agreements that provide for a bonus tied to the financial performance of the business during the year. Cash bonuses, like salary, are generally deductible by the business and taxable as ordinary income to the recipient of the bonus.

Stock Bonuses. Although bonuses are often paid in cash, some businesses provide bonuses in the form of stock. For example, if Owl Bookstore has grown over the years to become a national chain, it may wish to provide special recognition to Jane Smith, who has served Owl loyally as its chief financial officer since the business began. Accordingly, the board of directors may authorize Owl to issue a specified number of shares of stock to Jane in recognition of her past services and as an incentive to continue such exemplary performance in the future. The value of such a bonus depends, of course, on the value of the stock in Owl.

Both a business and its employee(s) should consider the tax, accounting and securities implications of a bonus payment that takes the form of an award of stock. For example, unless the stock has been registered under applicable federal and state securities laws, it may constitute "restricted" stock and be resalable only in compliance with applicable securities laws. As discussed in chapter three, restricted securities generally may be resold only after the passage of a three-year waiting period.

Determining how much stock in your business to give your employees as a bonus is a "business," not a legal, decision. Many (perhaps most) family business owners never give bonuses in the form of stock because they prefer not to dilute their ownership interest in their business. If you do choose to give a stock bonus, you should recognize that the number of shares issued as a bonus should be determined by considering the number of shares outstanding. For example, issuance of one share of stock in your business to a valued employee would represent 10 percent of the business if the business had only nine shares of stock previously outstanding, but would represent only 1 percent of the business if the business had ninety-nine shares of stock previously outstanding. In short, because shares of stock reflect a percentage ownership interest in a business, you will want to make sure that your employee's bonus reflects the intended percentage interest you choose to give away.

Health Insurance

Insurance is a valuable benefit that businesses often provide to their employees. The cost of medical and dental treatment is exceedingly high and seems to be rising rapidly each year. Although many businesses have historically paid the full cost of medical and dental insurance, many businesses are now passing along a portion of the insurance premiums to their employees.

COBRA. Business owners and their employees should be aware of their rights and responsibilities under the Consolidated Omnibus Budget Reconciliation Act of 1985 (COBRA). Under COBRA, certain group medical plans are required to permit continuation of medical coverage to "qualified beneficiaries" (e.g., employees, spouses and dependent children) upon the occurrence of certain events, such as death of the employee, divorce of the employee or termination of the employee's employment. These qualified beneficiaries may be required to pay the premiums on their insurance in order to continue their coverage.

Stock Options

One approach that many businesses, large and small, use to reward employees is the grant of stock options. A stock option is a contractual right granted by a corporation to an employee or other person to purchase a specified number of shares of the corporation's stock on or prior to a specified date at a specified purchase price. Until an employee exercises a stock option (and thereby acquires the stock subject to the option), he does not own the stock and has no rights as a shareholder. For example, Owl Bookstores, Inc. may grant a valued employee the right to purchase one hundred shares of Owl common stock at a price of $1 per share at any time during the ten-year period following the date of grant. If the price of Owl stock rises above $1 per share, the employee will have an incentive to exercise the option, thereby paying the (bargain) price of $1 per share.

The employee ordinarily may sell the stock purchased pursuant to an option agreement at any time and so, perhaps, make a nice profit. The employee's ability to sell the stock will, of course, require compliance with applicable securities laws and any contractual restrictions (such as a right-of-first-refusal) imposed on the employee by the company. By awarding stock options to a valued employee, an employer gives the employee an incentive to stay with the company and continue contributing to the appreciation in the value of the business.

Stock options come in a variety of forms. Many stock options do not vest (i.e., are not exercisable) on the date they are granted. Rather, they vest over a specified number of years. For example, an employee may be granted a stock option at the time he commences employment although the company may provide that the employee can only exercise the stock option (and hence acquire the stock subject to the option) if he remains employed by the company for a five-year period. In short, stock options are a way to use equity in a business to reward a valued employee and encourage the employee to continue to make a contribution to the business.

Nonqualified vs. Incentive. Stock options come in a variety of forms including the most common form known as "nonqualified stock options" or "incentive stock options." As a rule, an employee who exercises a stock option will realize ordinary income in the year he exercises the option in an amount equal to the difference between the market price of the stock acquired upon exercise and the exercise price. For example, if John Smith acquires one hundred shares of common stock of Owl Bookstore at a price of $1 per share at a time when the market value of the stock is $10 per share, Smith will realize ordinary income of $900. In contrast, an employee exercising an incentive stock option will generally not recognize income in the year the option is exercised, but will recognize income in the year he disposes of the stock acquired upon exercise of the option. Depending on the circumstances, such income may constitute capital gains, rather than ordinary income. Because employers who grant incentive stock options are not entitled to the same deductions available to employers who grant nonqualified stock options, any employer granting stock options should first consult with its attorney or accountant to develop an understanding of the tax and accounting treatment of the option grant and exercise. In this regard, special attention should be paid to the tax withholding obligations of an employee when an employee exercises an option and thereby recognizes ordinary income.

Termination of Option. It is important to clearly identify those circumstances that will lead to a termination of a stock option. If a person holding an option to buy stock in your business becomes disabled, dies or for any reason ceases to be an employee, you will probably not want him (or his estate) to have the ability to exercise the option. Similarly, if the shareholders of your business have entered into a shareholders' agreement imposing restrictions on the transfer of shares, you will want to make sure that any recipient of a stock option is subject to such agreement when he acquires stock upon exercise of the option.

Although granting stock or stock options to valued employees may be a good way to encourage diligence and loyalty, owners of family businesses may be reluctant to "give away" their business. If a decision is made to provide some or all employees with stock options, the family may want to retain the ability to repurchase the stock of the employee (perhaps at a premium price) in order to retain control of the business with the family. Other concerns noted in the context of granting stock to employees as a bonus may be applicable in this context as well.

Perquisites

Businesses often provide valuable nonmonetary benefits ("perquisites") to valued employees, such as purchasing club memberships and paying for or providing automobiles. Provision of such "perks" may not only keep a valued employee happy, but may make him a better employee, perhaps by enabling him to better "network" with potential customers.

☞ *STRATEGIC TIP*

A business should consider selecting perquisites that will further not just the interests of the employee but those of the business as well. For example, a business may choose to purchase a country club membership for an employee because the employee may have the opportunity to network at the club and thereby promote the products and services of the business to other club members. By purchasing the club membership for the employee, the business is not only compensating the employee, but also purchasing valuable publicity for itself.

Vacation

Businesses generally provide employees from one to four weeks of vacation annually (without diminution in salary as a result of the vacation time). In order to minimize disruption due to an extended absence, many businesses find it useful to restrict an employee's ability to take vacation time for more than two weeks in succession.

If your business is seasonal, make sure the employees know it and advise them at the outset of their employment that vacations during the peak season will be discouraged or not allowed. Family members who are employed by the business should be encouraged to respect the company-wide standard vacation policy and not take excessive vacations merely because they are "owners." By taking excessive vacation time, family employees may create jealousy and resentment among nonfamily employees. They may also disrupt business operations (for example, by being absent when needed for an important decision). Such disruption may have a variety of adverse effects and may, of course, be unfair to nonfamily-member shareholders who receive no salary (or vacation time!) but, instead, rely on their employees to earn their pay to create dividends for them as owners.

Retirement Benefits

Retirement benefits come in many forms and generally consist of defined contributions plans and defined benefit plans. In a defined contribution plan, a specified amount is contributed to a pension plan and the actual amount available to the employee-beneficiary depends on the investment performance of the plan. A defined benefit plan, in contrast, is a plan that provides the employee-beneficiary with a specified benefit amount (typically in the form of a cash contribution). To the extent that the investments of amounts contributed to the defined benefit plan do not achieve the assumed performance levels, the employer may be responsible for contributing additional amounts to the plan.

There are many retirement plan programs available, some of which are simple and others which are complicated to implement. We suggest that you consult with a person who specializes in employee benefits before determining what type of retirement plan(s) you will provide to your employees.

COMPENSATION POLICY

As a rule, the board of directors establishes compensation policies for the business, but as the business grows and hires more employees, the responsibility for setting compensation policies is generally divided between the board and certain executive officers (i.e., president and vice president). Then, the board usually will establish compensation arrangements for itself and for senior executives, but will delegate to senior executives responsibility for establishing compensation levels for nonexecutive employees. A board of directors owes a fiduciary duty to the shareholders of a corporation and, accordingly, may authorize payment of only fair (not exorbitant) salaries to employees. Payment of excessive salaries may result in a disgruntled shareholder filing a lawsuit against the directors for breach of fiduciary duty.

Decision Making

There is no right or wrong way for making compensation decisions, and yet, perhaps, no area of your business operations is more likely to lead to disputes and a subsequent deterioration of morale than the area of compensation. As long as people view their relative worth differently, either in terms of their talents, their efforts, or the value they add to the business, disputes will arise. Whatever approach a business takes to compensation decisions, the goal is clear: to establish a compensation program that both the employees and owners believe fairly distributes the money generated from the business.

To the extent that the business is able to identify a set of criteria that will govern compensation, the likelihood of dissension is reduced because employees understand in advance the "rules of the game." In addition, many businesses find it helpful to ask employees to evaluate themselves in order to facilitate compensation decisions. Although employees obviously have a tendency to be self-serving in their evaluations, the process can be helpful for several reasons. First, it may help senior management develop an appreciation of how the employee views his contributions to the business. Second, it may make the employee feel like he is a part of a critical aspect of the business. Third, it may enable an employee to examine his contributions critically and thereby grow and improve.

Compensation programs should be regularly reviewed to ensure that the criteria used for awarding compensation continue to be appropriate in light of the changing needs of the business and the ongoing contributions of employees.

☞ *STRATEGIC TIP*

It is worth noting that some people value job security (which is a form of compensation) more highly than salary increases, whereas other people are more concerned about their salary. Accordingly, you should try to keep a handle on the values your co-owners and/ or employees may have in order to help guide your decisions.

OWNERS VERSUS EMPLOYEES

A frequent source of dispute in the family business is the differing interests of owners and employees. Where one faction of a family controls the board of directors in a corporation, it may provide jobs or more generous salaries only to members of its faction and no jobs or less generous salaries to members of the other family faction. The result, of course, is that those family members who have not been given any "plum" jobs (or no jobs at all) may actually be or feel that they are compensated only through dividends. The problem may become further complicated because the business may have little or no money left to pay dividends because of the unreasonably high salaries paid to the family members with the "plum" jobs. For example, assume that two brothers, John and Paul, started Owl Bookstore forty years ago as equal owners. Today, Owl has twenty-five stores and net sales of $10 million annually. In 1993, John gives all of his stock in Owl to his three children and Paul gives one-third of his stock to his child, one-third of his stock to his church and the remaining one-third of his stock to four friends. If John's children vote their stock as a "block," they may be able to elect only themselves to the board of directors, and so could control the employment decisions of the business. These children may decide to employ themselves at generous salaries but not offer jobs to any of the other owners. If their salaries are high enough, little or no money will remain at the end of the year to pay dividends to the shareholders. Accordingly, the successor owners of Paul's stock, who may have little hope of receiving any present return on their stock, may be the owners of practically worthless stock (which may become valuable if and only if the business is one day sold).

A shareholders' or partnership agreement can be an effective mechanism by which minority shareholders or partners can protect themselves from being "squeezed out" from the financial fruits of their business. As indicated in chapter four, shareholders and partnership agreements should be executed at the start of a business so as to define and protect the rights and responsibilities of the shareholders or partners.

☞ *STRATEGIC TIP*

For a variety of reasons, one family member (or faction of a family) may choose to sell his ownership interest(s) in the family business yet remain involved as an employee. This development may work smoothly and fairly to everyone's advantage—or it may not. On occasion, the remaining owners may choose to make the former owner's life as an employee miserable. For example, the former owner may be given a new (smaller) office and have his secretary taken away, and the former perquisites he enjoyed (such as country club memberships) may be discontinued. In order to protect against such unplanned and undesirable developments, the selling owner may (if he wishes to remain as an employee) condition the buy-out agreement on a number of items that will bear on his upcoming status as a nonowner employee. Frequently, the more detail that is included in such agreements specifying what rights and perquisites will be available to the employee, the less likely disputes are to arise.

Chapter Seven

Selling (or Buying) Your Family Business

I n general, a family business may be started in one of two ways: One or more family members may start a brand new business, or they may acquire an existing business. For example, John Smith may begin a new business by incorporating Owl Bookstore, Inc., leasing retail space, entering into supply contracts with book publishers, hiring one or two employees and, so, beginning a business for the sale of books that previously did not exist. Alternatively, John Smith could buy an existing bookstore that has previously been owned by someone else.

Some owners have sought a middle ground between starting a business from scratch and purchasing an existing business — acquiring a franchise. A person who acquires a franchise (known as a "franchisee") purchases the right to operate a business under an established trademark and in accordance with an established format. McDonald's and Burger King are two of the best-known franchise operations.

The decision to start a business from scratch, to purchase an existing business, or to acquire a franchise will be influenced by a number of factors, including the availability, the cost, and the required expertise associated with each alternative.

Also, for a variety of reasons, the family business may be sold one day. Perhaps there is an opportunity to receive an attractive price for the business; perhaps no family member is interested in continuing to run it; perhaps the family is wracked by dissension and family members agree to sell the business. At that time, the family will want to make sure that the sale is completed on the most favorable terms possible.

This chapter considers some of the most important issues which the family must address when buying or selling its business. We treat these subjects together because these issues are the same for both a buyer and seller of a business (although, of course, their goals and interests are different). We believe that by addressing the basic issues involved in both purchasing and selling a business, the discussion should be clearer and more meaningful.

ESTABLISHING A PRICE FOR YOUR BUSINESS

A host of threshold questions arise in the purchase and sale of a business, but none is more important to the buyer and seller than the purchase price. A variety of factors affecting the purchase price should be considered.

Purchase Price

A buyer and seller must be able to establish the amount of the purchase price of a business. Obviously, there will be "no deal" if the buyer and seller cannot agree on the price of the business. Often, the price is based on comparable prices for similar businesses, a multiple of the book value of the business, the cash flow of the business which can be used to pay the purchase price (a so-called "leveraged buyout"), instinct, and/or some combination of these and other factors.

Impasse. Occasionally, a buyer and seller will be unable to agree upon the amount of the purchase price. The seller, pointing to his knowledge about the business, may have an optimistic view as to the prospects of continued growth for the business, whereas the buyer may be reluctant to pay a (premium) purchase price which reflects the seller's optimism.

A creative solution to overcoming an impasse on price might be to provide for a post-sale upward or downward adjustment in the amount of the purchase price based on the post-sale performance of the business. This solution requires resolution of a number of questions, including: (1) What are the targets that must be achieved by the business before the buyer will become obligated to pay an additional sum to the seller (and over what period of time must the buyer pay any such additional sum)? (2) If the business fails to achieve the targets, when will the seller return a portion of the purchase price to the buyer? (3) Once the seller has sold the business, how can he be sure that the buyer will operate the business efficiently so as to ensure that the agreed-upon targets will be achieved? and (4) How will disputes be resolved (and by whom) in the event that the seller and buyer disagree as to whether the targets have been met?

The seller and purchaser will need to focus on these and other ramifications in order to determine whether use of this "creative solution" makes sense in their particular circumstances. A satisfactory balance can often be struck between the simple and the complex approaches to reaching a business agreement, each of which has its respective costs and benefits.

☞ *STRATEGIC TIP*

Many creative approaches to paying (and being paid) the purchase price, and securing payment of the purchase price, have developed over the years, and the seller and buyer would each be well advised to discuss these approaches with their respective legal counsel before reaching a purchase and sale agreement.

Form of Payment

A purchase price for a business can take various forms, including (1) cash; (2) secured or unsecured promissory notes; (3) stock of the buyer; (4) noncash assets of the buyer (e.g., a swap of property); (5) an assumption by the buyer of liabilities of the seller; and (6) a combination of some or all of the foregoing.

The *amount* of the purchase price cannot meaningfully be determined independently of the *form* in which the purchase price will be paid. For example, two buyers may offer to pay $1,000,000 for your business. One buyer may offer to pay the $1,000,000 in cash at the time of the acquisition. The other buyer may offer to pay only $200,000 in cash at the time of the acquisition with the balance of the purchase price to be paid over the following five years in accordance with the terms of a promissory note. Which deal is better for you as the seller may, all else being equal, depend on the terms of the promissory note. If the promissory note is unsecured and bears interest at only 5 percent, the "all cash" deal is probably better. If the promissory note is fully secured by collateral (such as the assets of the business being purchased) and bears interest at 15 percent, you may be better off by selling your business for only $200,000 in cash and receiving payments on the 15 percent promissory note over the next five years.

A seller typically prefers to receive all of the purchase price in cash at the time of the sale since he thereby avoids (1) the risk of the buyer's nonpayment of future amounts otherwise due and (2) any need to value the "noncash" component of the purchase price. A buyer who is willing to pay the purchase price in cash may, accordingly, be able to get a better deal for the business than a buyer unable to pay cash up front. A buyer who is able to pay cash up front should consider insisting upon depositing a portion of the cash with a third-party (i.e., neutral) escrow agent who will return some or all of the cash in the event that the seller has breached any of his representations, warranties or agreements pertaining to the business. If, after the passage of an agreed-upon period of time, perhaps one year, it appears that the seller's representations and warranties were truthful and the seller has faithfully performed his agreements, the portion of the purchase price held in escrow may then be paid over to the seller. This escrow arrangement can provide the cash buyer with an added measure of protection.

WHAT'S FOR SALE?

Whether you structure the sale or acquisition of your business with the assets or stock of your business or as a merger, you must first determine what, specifically, is being bought or sold. For example, will a buyer purchase all of the manufacturing equipment currently being used by a seller or only the most modern equipment owned by the seller? Will a buyer or seller be responsible for the existing liabilities of the business? If John Smith wants to buy a competitor's book business, does he want to make the competitor's warehouse part of the deal or does John already have sufficient warehouse space? As the following discussion reveals, the determination of "what's for sale" is ultimately a function of the purchase (or sale) price of the business.

Assets to Be Purchased

An integral part of the decision to acquire or sell a business is the identification of the business assets which will be bought or sold. The parties are free to pick and choose among the assets of a business which will be included in the sale. As a general rule, the buyer will want to make sure that the assets he acquires will be sufficient to enable him to operate the business in the manner contemplated. If the seller desires to retain certain assets used in the business, the buyer may seek to negotiate a reduction in the purchase price in order to compensate him for the cost he will incur in acquiring the assets excluded from the sale.

☞ *STRATEGIC TIP*

A buyer should focus not simply on the tangible (hard) assets he will need to operate the business, but on the intangible assets, such as contract rights, as well. For example, can the seller's below-market lease be assigned? Will favorable supply contracts continue after the sale? Will the seller agree not to compete with the buyer for a period of time following the sale? In short, the buyer should consider what types of relations he would like to have once he acquires the business in order to evaluate whether contracts should be prepared to preserve the seller's existing relationships. Many buyers have been disappointed to discover that their sellers set up competing businesses following the sale and they have no legal recourse to prevent such competition.

Liabilities to Be Assumed

When a buyer agrees to assume some or all of the liabilities of the seller, the buyer, in effect, agrees to take over responsibilities which would otherwise have been the seller's. Accordingly, if a buyer assumes a seller's liability, the purchase price for the business should, in theory, be reduced. Stated differently, the real purchase price to a buyer of a business consists of the cash (and other property) to be paid to the seller *plus* the amount of the seller's liabilities being assumed. For example, if John Smith agrees to purchase all of the assets of Owl Bookstore from Jane Johnson, the current owner, for $500,000 and to assume Johnson's obligation to pay $15,000 in delinquent bills to suppliers, the *effective* (total) purchase price is $515,000.

Fixed and Contingent Liabilities. Certain liabilities of a business are fixed (such as an obligation to pay accrued taxes, employee salaries and rent for space being leased), whereas other liabilities are contingent (such as an obligation to refund a customer's money if, but only if, he seeks to return defective merchandise). In negotiating a purchase or sale price for the business, it may be difficult to determine how much a buyer's purchase price should be reduced in exchange for the buyer's agreement to assume a contingent liability. In lieu of seeking a reduction in the purchase price, a buyer may seek the seller's agreement to indemnify him (i.e., hold him harmless) in the event that the buyer later becomes obligated to pay a contingent liability. For example, John Smith may be willing to acquire Owl Bookstore from Jane Johnson for $500,000 in cash today plus an additional $400,000 payable with interest over a four-year period. Smith may also be prepared to assume Johnson's obligation to pay a total of $200,000 of identified liabilities to book suppliers and current employees. Finally, Johnson may have alerted Smith to the fact that several lawsuits have been brought against Owl Bookstore (for personal injuries caused by books falling on customers) which could result in liability. In determining how to account for these lawsuits, which may be won or lost (one form of contingent liability), the parties may, for example, choose to negotiate whether Smith should be responsible for (a) any and all of such contingent liability; (b) all of such liability up to, but not exceeding, an agreed-upon dollar ceiling; (c) only such liability as exceeds an agreed-upon threshold dollar amount; or (d) only such liability as exceeds an agreed-upon threshold dollar amount but does not exceed an agreed-upon dollar ceiling. A failure of the buyer and seller to address such matters clearly in advance of the closing of the purchase and sale will inevitably lead to disputes after the closing.

☞ STRATEGIC TIP

If you are selling your business, consider insisting that you only bear the responsibility for liabilities which exceed an agreed-upon threshold dollar amount, so as not to be "nickled and dimed" by the buyer for every minor problem.

OPTIONS FOR STRUCTURING YOUR DEAL

The form in which an acquisition is structured helps determine which assets will be included and which liabilities will be assumed as part of the sale of the business. The three most common forms of acquisition are (1) an acquisition of a business's assets; (2) an acquisition of a business's stock; and (3) a merger. Each of these forms is considered below.

Asset Acquisition

In an *asset* acquisition, only those assets which are expressly identified by the buyer and seller will be included in, and made a part of, the sale. In addition, with limited exceptions, only those liabilities which the buyer expressly agrees to assume will be included in the sale and, so, become the buyer's legal responsibility.

☞ STRATEGIC TIP

Certain liabilities become the buyer's responsibility regardless of whether or not he has contractually agreed to assume them. For example, courts have held a buyer of assets of a business liable for obligations of the business even though the buyer did not agree to, and did not intend to, assume such liabilities where (1) the sale is a fraudulent attempt by the seller to escape debts and liabilities; (2) a specific statute automatically imposes liability on the buyer (such as certain federal environmental laws which impose "clean-up" liability on owners and operators of contaminated land regardless of whether or not they were responsible for causing the contamination; or (3) developing public policies seeks to shift the cost of accidents to the parties considered to be in the best position to reduce the incidence of accidents and to bear the cost of an accident if it occurs. You should consider with your attorney the possible unintended liabilities you may face as buyer of a business in order to know more precisely what you are acquiring.

If a buyer is unaware that he is assuming responsibility as a matter of law for certain liabilities that he has not expressly agreed to assume, he may inadvertently fail to negotiate either a contractual right to indemnification from the seller or a reduction in the purchase price of the business to compensate him for assuming responsibility for such liabilities. Accordingly, such a buyer may find (to his dismay) that the acquired business is not as profitable as he had hoped it would be. We recommend that a buyer conduct a thorough investigation of a business (a "due diligence" investigation) before buying it to minimize the likelihood that he will discover liabilities only after he has become responsible for discharging them.

Stock Acquisition

In a *stock* acquisition, the buyer acquires the stock of a corporation from the existing shareholder(s) of the corporation. In a stock acquisition, all of the acquired corporation's assets and liabilities remain with, and as part of, the corporation; only the ownership of the corporation changes.

The selling shareholder(s) and the buyer are free, of course, to agree in advance of the purchase and sale of the stock to "remove" from the corporation certain assets. Accordingly, the fact that a transaction is structured as a sale of stock need not limit the ability of the parties to define or limit the specific business which will be transferred to the buyer upon sale of the stock.

Multiple Shareholders. If two or more people own the stock of a corporation, the buyer will only be able to acquire all of the stock if (1) each shareholder voluntarily agrees to sell his stock to the buyer; (2) each shareholder is contractually obligated (for example, by a shareholders' agreement) to sell his stock to the buyer; or (3) a majority or, depending on the laws of the applicable state, two-thirds of the shareholders approve a merger, which is discussed below. You should consider the *practicality* of acquiring complete ownership of a business as soon as possible to avoid wasted time and effort.

In addition, if a buyer intends to buy the stock of a corporation from two or more people, the buyer should exact the *commitment* of each of the selling stockholders to agree in principle to the sale of his stock early on so as to minimize the likelihood that one of the sellers will back out of the deal at the last minute. Accordingly, the buyer should attempt to negotiate a purchase agreement early on, but condition his obligation to close under the agreement until after his "due-diligence" investigation of the business has been completed.

Merger

A merger is a transaction governed by state law. There are two common types of merger—a "two-party" merger and a "three-party" merger.

Two-party Merger. In a two-party merger, one corporation is combined into another corporation and its separate corporate existence ceases. All of the assets and liabilities of the "disappearing corporation" become the assets and liabilities of the "surviving corporation." The purchase price paid to the shareholders of the disappearing corporation can consist of cash, indebtedness or securities of the surviving corporation or its affiliate(s). For example, if Jane's Bookstore, Inc. ("JBI") is merged into Owl Bookstore, JBI will cease to exist as of the effective date of the merger, and the former shareholders of JBI will, in exchange for their stock in

JBI, receive the agreed upon purchase price. Upon JBI's merger into Owl Bookstore, all of JBI's assets and liabilities become Owl Bookstore's assets and liabilities.

Three-Party Merger. A buyer may not want to directly assume all of the liabilities of the corporation it is seeking to acquire. It may want to keep such liabilities segregated in a separate corporation. In a three-party (or "triangular") merger, a subsidiary of the buyer is used to acquire the seller. In a "forward triangular merger," the seller is merged into a subsidiary of the buyer and the subsidiary's corporate existence continues, with the result that the buyer's subsidiary acquires all of the assets and becomes subject to all of the liabilities of the seller. Alternatively, the buyer's subsidiary can be merged into the seller so that the original subsidiary of the buyer disappears and the seller becomes a wholly owned subsidiary of the buyer. This latter type of triangular merger, known as a "reverse triangular merger," allows the buyer to acquire all of the stock of the seller while preserving the seller's separate and continuing corporate existence.

SELECTING THE RIGHT STRUCTURE

Whether a business should be bought or sold by an asset or stock acquisition or by a conventional or triangular merger will depend on the buyer's and seller's objectives and constraints. Some of the most common objectives and constraints include:

Minimizing Tax Liability

The buyer's and seller's desire to minimize their respective tax liability commonly influences the structure selected. Certain acquisitions can be accomplished as tax-free "reorganizations" if properly structured. A tax-free reorganization does not allow a seller to escape taxable gain it realizes from a sale of its business, but it can permit such gain to be deferred until a later date. In addition, in an assets acquisition, the buyer is generally entitled to "write up" the value of the acquired assets based on the purchase price and thereby acquire a higher tax basis in the assets than the assets had prior to the sale. Such a write-up will enable the buyer to minimize tax liability in future years by depreciating or "writing down" these assets over time. For example, Owl Bookstore may have acquired one hundred bookshelves in 1965 for $5,000. This business expense may have been used in the following years to reduce the business's taxable income (through "depreciation"). Indeed, at the time of the sale of Owl Bookstore to John Smith in 1993, the bookshelves may have been completely "written off" for tax purposes. If Smith were to buy the stock of Owl, he would generally *not* be able to write up the value of the bookshelves to their fair market value. Rather, he would acquire the business without changing the depreciable basis of the assets of the business. In contrast, if Smith were to buy the assets of Owl, including making a $5,000 payment for the one hundred bookshelves, he would probably be entitled to write up the tax basis of the bookshelves and then be able to depreciate them all over again to reduce his business's future tax liability.

Minimizing Exposure to Liabilities

The buyer's and seller's desire to minimize their respective liability exposure commonly influences the acquisition structure selected. For example, a buyer may desire to acquire a business engaged in manufacturing hazardous products, such as rifles, for a purchase price of $500,000. The business faces potentially enormous liability claims if its products cause personal injuries to its customers or innocent third parties. If, for example, a rifle explodes when fired, the customer or a third party may be severely injured or even killed. The buyer may be prepared to risk the loss of his $500,000 investment in the rifle business but may not be prepared to risk all of his other assets to satisfy potential liability claims (especially claims that relate to activities occurring before the date the business is acquired).

If the buyer acquires the assets and assumes the liabilities of the business (or, as discussed below, in the context of a corporate buyer, merges the seller directly into itself), the buyer would be directly exposed to any damages resulting from a product liability suit. Such exposure may be acceptable to the buyer, especially if the buyer has been formed as a corporation in order to afford its stockholders limited liability. If, however, the buyer acquires the stock of the business directly from the shareholders or pursuant to a triangular merger, the buyer (whether or not organized as a corporation) would be afforded the benefit of limited liability enjoyed by shareholders of a corporation. If the acquired business suffers a major loss, the value of the buyer's $500,000 investment in the business will, of course, be diminished, but the buyer will generally not be liable to pay any losses incurred by the acquired business in excess of the assets of the business.

Avoiding Loss of Valuable Contract Rights

A buyer's desire to avoid losing valuable contract rights held by a seller can also influence selection of the structure of the purchase and sale. For example, a seller may have entered into a long-term lease for real estate at a rental level substantially below current market rental levels. The lease agreement may give the landlord the right to terminate the lease if all or a substantial part of the seller's business assets are sold. The buyer may, nevertheless, be able to acquire the business while avoiding loss of the valuable "below-market" lease simply by acquiring from the shareholders the stock of the business that entered into the lease. Unless the lease gives the landlord the right to terminate the lease upon a change in the ownership of the business (as opposed to simply a sale of the assets of the business), a sale of stock can ensure retaining this valuable lease. For example, assume that Owl Bookstore, Inc. entered into a lease in 1992 for 100,000 square feet of retail space at a rental of $17 per square foot in 1993. The lease may restrict Owl's right to assign or sublet the leased property. However, the lease may not restrict the ability of the owners of Owl Bookstore, Inc. from selling their stock in Owl to a third party.

Circumventing Obstructionist Shareholders

There are occasions when minority shareholders of a business seek to block a sale of their business for inappropriate reasons (such as malice or spite). Selecting a particular structure may make it easier for the majority owners to pursue their desired course of action. For example, Owl Bookstore may be owned by three shareholders who each own a one-third interest in the corporation. Two of the shareholders, John and Amy Smith, desire to sell Owl and one shareholder, Joe Stubborn, prefers not to sell. Assume that Linda Jones wishes to buy Owl but only if she can acquire complete ownership and thereby have the flexibility to operate Owl as she sees fit. In such a scenario, a stock acquisition is not possible since, absent a contractual arrangement entered into by the shareholders, Joe cannot be forced to sell his shares to Linda or any other buyer, even if Linda were to offer Joe a premium for his stock. However, most states provide that a *merger* can be effected if more than a majority (or, in some states, two-thirds) of the outstanding shareholders of stock approve the merger. Accordingly, the buyer (Linda) can arrange with John and Amy to approve the merger in accordance with the required formalities of state law and then merge Owl into an appropriate entity owned by Linda. After the merger, Joe Stubborn, who opposed the acquisition, will no longer have an ownership interest in Owl. Joe will only be entitled to receive the consideration provided for in the merger.

☞ *STRATEGIC TIP*

Every state law provides that shareholders who oppose a merger and who follow certain prescribed steps can have a court determine the fair value of their shares and receive such value in cash in lieu of receiving the consideration otherwise available as a result of the merger. Such "dissenting shareholders" may exercise certain rights which are generally known as "Rights of Appraisal."

REPRESENTATIONS AND WARRANTIES

Scope

Often, when property is bought and sold, a seller may not make (nor may a buyer expect a seller to make) any representations or warranties as to the fitness or qualities of the objects. For example, when a house is sold, the seller typically does not make any representations or warranties as to the condition of the house, its general suitability or its limited suitability for any particular purpose. If the buyer is concerned, he may engage an inspector at his expense to inspect the house in order to make sure that the house contains no defects other than those of which he has knowledge.

In contrast, when a business is sold, the buyer typically insists that the seller make numerous representations and warranties pertaining to the business. The scope of the representations and warranties typically is a function of the buyer's and seller's relative negotiating strength and the extent to which the buyer wants or requires contractual assurances from the seller with respect to particular aspects of the business.

☞ *STRATEGIC TIP*

The following are some of the more important subjects which, as a buyer, you might reasonably require representations and warranties about from the seller:

1. the due organization of the seller (assuming the seller is a corporation, limited partnership, or the like)
2. the seller's authorization to sell the business
3. the absence of any governmental or third-party consents or approvals required to consummate the sale
4. the seller's title to its assets and its right to sell the assets
5. the quality and adequacy of the assets owned by the seller, with specific representations tailored to inventory (e.g., that the inventory is not obsolete), accounts receivable (e.g., that the accounts receivable are collectable in the ordinary course of business), equipment, vehicles, information systems, patents and any other relevant category of assets owned by the seller
6. whether the seller's business has been operated in compliance with all applicable laws and with all contracts to which it is a party
7. whether the seller's business is involved in litigation or whether any lawsuits have been threatened
8. whether the seller has paid all applicable taxes
9. whether the seller has maintained good relations with its employees, suppliers and customers
10. whether any material changes have occurred in the business since the date of the seller's latest financial statements
11. whether the seller's business is subject to any claims or liabilities other than those set forth in the seller's financial statements and
12. whether the seller's business has adequate insurance.

Qualifications

Even if the seller and buyer are able to agree on the *subjects* about which the seller will make representations and warranties, they then must agree as to the *scope* of the representations and warranties and of any qualifications the seller would like to make to these representations and warranties.

For example, the seller may be *willing* to represent that all of his inventory was acquired within the past twelve months, but may be *unwilling* to represent that none of such inventory is obsolete. The seller may resist making this latter representation because of the difficulty of precisely defining the term "obsolete" and because this may require him to make a qualitative assessment as to the probable future demands of customers. The seller may argue that the buyer is equally capable of assessing how rapidly the inventory will be depleted in the course of operating the business. The buyer, of course, may lack the seller's experience with the business and will argue that the seller is adequately suited to provide such a representation.

The buyer may also ask the seller to represent that all of the seller's contracts are in full force and that such contracts have not been breached. The seller may agree to give this representation but, with respect to absence of breaches, seek to qualify it by reference to his actual knowledge as to action by third parties which may have created a breach of contract. For example, the seller may have unconditionally represented that he has not breached a particular contract, but only represent that, to his actual knowledge, the other party to the contract has not breached it.

One might reasonably ask whether all representations and warranties are, necessarily, either expressly or impliedly qualified by the knowledge of the party making the representation or warranty. The answer depends on what is, specifically, being represented or warranted.

On the one hand, a person may attempt to limit the scope of the term "knowledge" to *actual* knowledge rather than knowledge that a reasonable person may be presumed to have under the relevant circumstances.

On the other hand, a buyer's interest in the seller's representations and warranties about the business goes beyond mere curiosity about the "true nature" of the business. Indeed, representations and warranties are an important means to enable the buyer and seller to allocate future business risks. For example, assume that a buyer of a gun manufacturing business asks the seller to represent that "all of the guns sold by the business are free of defects." The seller may only represent that all of such guns are, to the seller's knowledge, "free of defects." The buyer would be seriously mistaken if he assumes that seller's "knowledge" qualification is irrelevant. For example, six months after the purchase and sale is completed, a gun, which was sold prior to the date the business was sold, explodes in the hand of a user. A court concludes that the gun was defective and awards a judgment against the business. As a result of the judgment, the buyer may claim that the seller's inaccurate representation justifies holding the seller responsible for the amount awarded by the judgment. The success of the buyer's claim will depend on which of two representations the seller made. If the seller represented that "all of the products sold by the business are, *to his knowledge*, free of defects," the buyer will not be able to claim that the seller breached his representation unless he can prove that the seller knew about the defects yet failed to disclose their existence to the buyer. If, however, the seller represented that "all of the products sold by the business *are free of defects*," the buyer will be able to claim that the seller breached his representation because at least one of the products sold by the business was, by definition, defective. Even though the seller had no knowledge of the defect, he assumed the risk of loss arising out of the defect. Accordingly, in negotiating representations and warranties, the buyer and seller should understand that they are engaged in a process of risk allocation and should negotiate the precise terms of such representations and warranties on the basis of only those risks they are prepared to accept.

☞ *STRATEGIC TIP*

A prospective buyer of your business may ask you to identify all lawsuits pending against your business. You may agree to make such a representation but be extremely careful before also representing the likelihood that the lawsuits will be resolved favorably to the business.

Survival Period

As part of the process of negotiating representations and warranties, the buyer and seller will need to agree as to the "survival" period of each representation or warranty. Unless otherwise expressly agreed to, representations and warranties may terminate after the sale of the business has occurred. The survival period which a buyer and seller may negotiate generally reflects the time period which they agree is reasonable to enable the buyer to acquire a good understanding of the operations and activities of the business in order to assess whether the representations and warranties are, in fact, accurate. For example, the parties may agree that all representations and warranties survive for one year following the closing. Following the first anniversary of the closing, no claims based on an inaccurate representation may be asserted, although any disputes over alleged inaccuracies asserted prior to the first anniversary may be resolved after the first anniversary. If the buyer is concerned that one year may not be adequate to enable him to discover inaccurate representations and warranties, he should seek a longer survival period. For example, buyers frequently require a seller's representation that the business has paid all of its taxes to survive until expiration of the applicable statute of limitations so that the buyer can be sure that it will have recourse against the seller in the event that the IRS or applicable state agency brings a claim for unpaid taxes.

Indemnification

In the event that any of the seller's representations and warranties about the business prove to be inaccurate and result in financial loss to the buyer or the purchased business, the buyer will want to have redress against the seller. Accordingly, most acquisition agreements contain an "indemnification" section. In the indemnification section, the seller agrees to hold the buyer harmless against any losses the buyer incurs as a result of an inaccurate representation or warranty or a breach by the seller of a specified contractual obligation.

Indemnification agreements are usually heavily negotiated and come in a variety of forms which you should consider with your attorney. For example, a seller may agree to indemnify a buyer only if a loss is discovered within one year of closing. In addition, a seller may agree to indemnify a buyer only to the extent losses exceed a specified dollar amount or do not exceed a specified dollar amount. The rationale frequently given for providing a "deductible" in an indemnification provision is that the seller ought not to be "nickeled and dimed" by the buyer for losses which are not, in and of themselves, significant.

A buyer of a business should bear in mind that an indemnification obligation is simply a promise by the seller to hold the buyer harmless under certain circumstances. Accordingly, an indemnification obligation is only as good as the word of the seller. To protect himself against a dishonest seller (or a seller without sufficient resources to back up his promises), a buyer of a business can insist upon "security" for a seller's indemnification obligation. The security frequently takes the form of a deposit of a portion of the purchase price into an escrow account. Only after a specified period of time has elapsed and the buyer has not discovered any inaccurate representations or warranties by the seller, will the amount deposited into escrow be released to the seller.

STEPS IN EFFECTING AN ACQUISITION

Although there are no fixed steps which must be taken in completing an acquisition, many acquisitions proceed as follows:

Letter of Intent

Generally, the first step in an acquisition is to negotiate the terms of a letter of intent. Letters of intent may be "binding" or "nonbinding," but each form generally prohibits the seller from entertaining other bids for the business for a specified period of time. Most letters of intent set forth the general terms of the purchase and sale. For example, most letters of intent specify the purchase price, the form of the sale (i.e., asset or stock sale or merger), and conditions to be satisfied in order to close the transaction.

Many letters of intent also obligate the parties to keep the purchase and sale negotiations confidential. From the seller's perspective, premature disclosure of an impending sale of a business can be very disruptive for suppliers and employees of the business. From the buyer's perspective, premature disclosure of the negotiations can be detrimental because it may alert other potential buyers about a good acquisition opportunity. These potential buyers could bid against the buyer for the business and thereby raise the ultimate purchase price paid or even then acquire the business.

Documentation

After signing a letter of intent, the buyer and seller (and their respective attorneys) will begin to prepare documentation setting forth the terms upon which the business will be sold. The documentation can be elaborate or simple, depending upon the parties' objectives. The documentation generally undergoes numerous changes as the parties negotiate an agreement that each believes accommodates its needs.

Due Diligence

A buyer of a business will generally conduct a thorough investigation of the business before it actually acquires the business. This investigation, commonly known as a "due diligence" investigation, not only enables a buyer to learn about the business and how it operates, but also to obtain comfort that the representations and warranties that the seller is making are true and correct.

Frequently, a buyer will, during the course of his due diligence investigation, discover aspects of a business of which he was previously unaware. The buyer may, following such discovery, seek to renegotiate the terms of the acquisition to reflect the new information.

Third-Party Consents

While due diligence is taking place and documents are being negotiated, the buyer and seller will seek to obtain any governmental or third-party consents that may be required as a condition to the sale. For example, a seller may need to obtain the consent of his creditors to a sale of the business. Frequently, consents of landlords will be required if the business being sold leases space from a third party and the prospective buyer wishes to continue using the space.

Financing Contingency

A buyer may require bank financing to pay for all or part of the purchase price and, without a bank's commitment to provide a loan to fund the acquisition, the sale may not occur. The buyer and the seller should carefully focus on their respective rights and obligations in order that they are not unduly disappointed in the event that the buyer is unable to obtain the necessary financing prior to the closing.

Closing

After the buyer has completed his due diligence investigation of the business, the documentation has been fully negotiated, all third-party consents have been obtained and any financing required by the buyer has been obtained, the parties will proceed to "close" the transaction. At the closing, instruments transferring the agreed upon stock and/or assets are executed pursuant to which the seller conveys his rights in the business to the buyer and the buyer pays the purchase price to the seller. Following the closing, the buyer will be the owner of the business.

Operating the Acquired Business

Once the buyer has acquired the business, he is ready to begin operating it. Often, the buyer has developed some expertise or acquired useful information over the course of the acquisition process which will permit him to operate the business more profitably. For example, the buyer may now have a better understanding of the relationship of the business to its suppliers and customers. Finally, the buyer will want to ensure that he has taken all other appropriate or required steps to help promote successful operations. For example, the buyer should have sufficient financing to pay ongoing operating expenses and should have lined up insurance coverage and have arranged for adequate staffing (i.e., employees) of the business.

MISCELLANEOUS ASPECTS OF ACQUISITIONS

The foregoing discussion should by no means be construed as exhaustive. Each acquisition is unique and raises special issues that must be addressed. For example, the buyer may recognize that the seller is a very experienced and savvy businessman. Accordingly, the buyer may seek a contractual condition which requires the seller to refrain from engaging in the same or similar business for several years following the closing. The geographic scope and duration of noncompetition agreements are often heavily negotiated but can prove critical to a successful business acquisition. Such noncompetition agreements can also provide tax benefits by enabling the buyer to "allocate" part of the purchase price to the noncompetition agreement which may provide a tax deduction.

☞ *STRATEGIC TIP*

Because of the complex issues that are invariably raised, you will want to consult with an attorney experienced in buying and selling businesses if (or when) you face this task.

Chapter Eight

Estate Planning and Your Business

Generally, estate planning involves the structuring of your personal and business affairs so that (1) you may maximize your wealth during your lifetime and (2) upon your death, your wealth may be distributed to your heirs with a minimum of estate tax. While the other chapters in this book are intended to help you learn to maximize your wealth by operating a successful family business, this chapter is specifically designed to offer you a variety of techniques which may help ensure the continuation of your family business upon your retirement or death and the lowest possible estate taxes.

Estate planning for a family business owner usually involves careful consideration of both business and personal objectives. For example, an owner of a family business may need to decide (1) how to provide for his children who are not active in the business; (2) how to provide for his surviving spouse—without having the spouse interfere with the business judgment of the children who are active in the business; or (3) which of two or more children should become the president of the business upon the founder's demise. As you can see, consideration of business objectives without personal objectives is insufficient, useless, or even counterproductive. Such a recognition is often difficult because it is not unusual for these two objectives to conflict. While each reader must inevitably resolve his estate planning objectives in his own style, for his own good reasons, the following discussion may help you identify and select the most desirable options from you and your family's point of view.

As a family business owner, estate planning does not merely involve selecting your heirs and making sure your will correctly reflects that selection. While that is, perhaps, satisfactory for other people in different circumstances, your estate planning considerations as an owner of a family business are more complex and challenging—yet more interesting as well. In order to understand which specific estate planning techniques may be useful to you, we believe you must first understand why certain factors make your planning more challenging and why these factors are ordinarily considered in estate planning for family business owners.

☞ *STRATEGIC TIP*

Most people dislike engaging in their own estate planning. A number of factors may explain this dislike. Perhaps most obvious is the fact that most of us simply do not like to consider our own mortality. Also, most of us prefer to avoid making the difficult decisions which estate planning often entails: how much control of my business should I give to my only son-in-law (who may one day divorce my daughter?); should one of my three children inherit a controlling interest in the business or should they inherit equal ownership interests? Others prefer privacy and control over business decisions and believe they would lose both by undertaking estate planning. Although these concerns are understandable, we urge you to put these concerns aside and begin your estate planning at once. You have worked hard to make your business a success and, with such planning, your heirs can benefit from your efforts. Without planning, you can jeopardize or destroy much of your life's efforts.

UNIQUE PLANNING CONCERNS FOR THE FAMILY BUSINESS OWNER

The Value of Your Business

While most of your assets may be easy to value, your family business may not be. For example, your car, coin collection, house and the like can all be readily valued by comparison to the existing markets for such items. If an identical house across the street from your house has just sold for $100,000, you may have good reason to believe that your house has roughly the same value. Even your ownership of certain business interests can be easily valued. For instance, shares of stock you own in "public corporations" are easy to value by reference to the stock market on which such shares are traded. Your family business, however, is different. If your family business has never "been on the market," establishing its realistic value may be difficult. How can you really be sure what someone might pay for it until you actually sell it in an "arm's-length" transaction?

☞ *STRATEGIC TIP*

Notwithstanding the difficulty of establishing the value of a family business, it must be done — and done at an early stage of your planning. Inevitably (typically upon your demise), the federal and state tax collectors will establish their "fair market value" of your family business so they can collect their estate taxes due. By estimating the value of your business now, you can estimate your estate's potential future tax bill. This projected bill will, in turn, help you plan to raise or save sufficient cash to pay this bill. This plan will also help you estimate how much "after tax wealth" your estate will have for your heirs.

The Internal Revenue Service has stated that the value of property may be defined as "the price at which the property would change hands between a willing buyer and a willing seller when the former is not under any compulsion to buy and the latter is not under any compulsion to sell, both parties having reasonable knowledge of relevant facts." (Revenue Ruling 59-60, 159-1 [13237]) It is often appropriate or necessary to retain an appraiser who is expert in valuing businesses in your industry to help you understand the value of your business. The fair market value of your business (or your fractional ownership interest therein) on your date of death is the value upon which your estate must pay estate taxes. Accordingly, if you start a business on a shoestring and, when you die, it is worth $1,000,000, your estate may owe the IRS up to $550,000! Obviously, effective planning requires you to learn the facts of your business.

Once a value for your business has been established, the IRS recognizes that it may then be appropriate to "discount" this value to reflect peculiar facts and circumstances which may make an ownership interest in your business worth less than an ownership interest in a similar business with different facts and circumstances. For example, a discount for *lack of marketability* is frequently applied to shares in family businesses to reflect the fact that there is no (or only a limited) market for such shares and, as a result, such shares are not readily transferable. Another type of discount is the so-called *minority discount* that reflects the fact that an owner of a minority interest in a business cannot control policy, cannot control distributions of funds (such as dividends) and cannot compel a liquidation of the business. These and other discounts may reduce the value of your interest in your family business below the value of the business as a whole. These discounts (which can range as high as 30 to 60 percent) are important because the deeper the discount, the lower the value of your business and, so, the lower your estate tax.

Wealth vs. Liquidity

Estate planning for family business owners is often complicated because of the difference between "wealth" and "liquidity." A person may be wealthy solely because the value of his family business is high. For example, if John Smith owns Owl Bookstore, which is valued at $1,000,000, he may be as wealthy as his sister Amy, who has $1,000,000 in cash on deposit in her bank. Amy, however, can quickly put her hands on her wealth (i.e., it can be easily liquidated) while John may never actually "convert" his wealth into actual cash. Rather than selling his business for cash, he may prefer to have his son and daughter continue to own and operate it. Accordingly, John's wealth may be considered "illiquid."

This distinction between wealth and liquidity plays an important role in estate planning for family business owners because, while most businesses are illiquid, *their values are estate taxable on the same basis and rates as liquid assets!* Thus, John and Amy may have identical estate tax bills upon their respective deaths, but only Amy's estate may be readily able to pay its bill. Unless John's heirs are prepared to sell Owl to raise cash to pay this bill, raising cash to pay tax collectors may be difficult or impossible. This problem explains the common complaint family business owners often make that the tax system literally forces them "out of business."

☞ *STRATEGIC TIP*

Insurance is often one useful means to help raise the necessary amount of liquidity to pay estate taxes without forcing the sale of a business. You and your heirs should exercise care in selecting the most useful kind of insurance to fit your specific needs. Indeed, some policies, if owned by your business, can actually exacerbate your estate tax problem because, when you die, your business may receive the cash proceeds due under the insurance contract—which can increase the value of your business and, so, the amount of estate tax due as a result of your ownership interest in the business! We suggest you consider purchasing insurance only from a reliable agent, experienced in the peculiar arena of business succession planning.

Business Continuity—The "Successorship" Question

Because of the distinction noted above between wealth and liquidity, it is not unusual for a family business owner to sell the business as he nears retirement. By "cashing out," an owner can help provide sufficient income for his retirement years and the availability of liquid assets to pay estate taxes due upon his death. Many owners, however, prefer to give their children the option of continuing the family business. Although this option may complicate the estate plan by limiting the most obvious source to raise cash to pay estate taxes—the business itself—the preference to turn the business over to their children or other heirs often outweighs this consideration. If the business is to be continued, an important and related "planning issue" must be resolved: Which of the owner's heirs will own the business and are they competent to manage it?

While this question does not necessarily implicate "legal" concerns, it is of critical importance to your estate planning. Unless the family business owner can find and train a competent successor to help ensure the continuing success of the business, the owner should rethink his good intentions of leaving his business for his heirs. Even the most profitable of businesses can quickly become bankrupt if an incompetent leader is at the helm. Tales of vast family fortunes lost virtually overnight as a result of incompetent successors are not unusual. Accordingly, the owner and family members should carefully consider what, if any, plans should be made for the future management of the business.

☞ STRATEGIC TIP

The family should not necessarily limit its consideration of potential management successors to family members. Valued employees or individuals with no prior connection to the business may need to be considered. Thought should be given to a variety of factors, including experience, education, opportunity for training, and personalities. How potential successors might "work together" should be taken into account. Many families have sought to avoid the potential for conflict by, for example, (1) limiting the number of successors by historical accident (e.g., only the first-born male child can continue in management); (2) dividing the business into several smaller new businesses so several successors can be selected; or (3) encouraging one potential successor to go into another respectable line of work (perhaps law!). We do not recommend that you blindly rely on any particular factor but, instead, suggest that you carefully consider each factor with your family and advisors to help ensure that an intelligent (and workable) plan of succession is chosen.

ESTATE AND GIFT TAX BASICS

The federal government (through the IRS) raises money by taxing the transfer of certain property. Taxes are imposed on (1) lifetime gifts, (2) estates upon an individual's death, and (3) certain "generation-skipping" transfers. These taxes can amount to 55 percent of the value of the gift, estate or transfer. In addition, many states impose their own (additional) estate tax. The following discussion explains why these various taxes require you to engage in very careful planning to reduce or even eliminate these various tax burdens so that you can help ensure the continuation of your family business upon your retirement or demise.

Up until now, we have generally referred to the estate tax bill that is payable upon an individual's demise. In order to effectively design an estate plan that is right for you, it is helpful to appreciate the basics of estate and gift taxation so your consultations with your professional advisors remain meaningful. This arena is complex and fraught with difficult issues. The following discussion is intended to give you a broad overview of the basics.

Estate Taxes

Depending on the size of your estate, the federal estate tax may be burdensome or outright confiscatory. Estates are taxed by the federal government in progressively increasing "tax brackets" which begin at 18 percent and, under the Revenue Reconciliation Act of 1993 (or the Omnibus Budget Reconciliation Act of 1993), rise up to 55 percent of the taxable estate. In addition, various states have their own estate taxes or inheritance taxes which can increase the tax bite even more. For example, because New York State has its own 5 percent estate tax, it is possible that larger estates are taxable at a 60 percent rate! The tax is levied upon all of the assets in your estate — liquid and illiquid assets alike — from cash in the bank to furniture in your guest room. Deductions are permitted for typically nominal expenses such as funeral and administrative expenses, claims and debts of the estate and certain state death taxes.

One of the most important deductions is found in Section 2056 of the Internal Revenue Code which authorizes an unlimited deduction for certain ("qualified") bequests to a surviving spouse. This "unlimited marital deduction" may allow you to pass all of the assets in your estate to your spouse free of tax. This deduction, does not, however, cancel the estate tax — it merely defers it to your spouse's death. If your assets appreciate in value after your death, the tax can actually be greater upon your spouse's death at a later date! In order to qualify for the unlimited marital deduction, your surviving spouse must be given either an unqualified ownership interest in your assets or a narrowly defined "qualified" interest. You will want to consider such qualifications with your attorney. Because the estate tax is so broad in its applicability and high in rate, careful planning is required to minimize its effect and, so, permit the transmission of your wealth and family business to your heirs.

Gift Tax

The Internal Revenue Code also imposes a tax "on the transfer of property by gift" made during each calendar year. A gift is generally defined to include the transfer of property without any consideration or for less consideration than the property is worth. The value of a gift is determined as of the date the gift is made. Computation of the gift tax is fairly complex and you should consider seeking professional advice to assist your planning. Essentially, gift tax is computed on the basis of all gifts made by the donor over the course of his lifetime. This cumulative tax requires that all taxable gifts be aggregated through the end of the taxable year and a tax then assessed on that amount. That amount, in turn, is reduced by the amount of tax paid on taxable gifts up to the beginning of the current year. The net amount is the amount of gift tax to be paid in the current tax year in which the gift is made. The progressive gift tax rates, like estate tax rates, may now reach a maximum rate of 55 percent!

An important exception to this gift tax is the so-called *annual exclusion* which permits every donor to give away up to $10,000 per donee every year. This annual exclusion, because of its importance to estate planning for business owners, is discussed in more detail below.

Unified Schedule for Estate and Gift Taxes

The Internal Revenue Code was changed in 1976 to integrate the various taxes imposed on gifts, estates and generation-skipping transfers. These various taxes are now all determined by reference to a "unified tax rate" (unlike in prior years during which separate rate schedules were used). Essentially, it is no longer possible to make lifetime gifts beyond allowable exclusions that remove the value of gifted property from the donor's taxable estate. This unified rate schedule is extremely complex in its application and you will want to discuss its usefulness with your professional advisors. A particularly important aspect of this unified tax system is the *unified credit* established by Internal Revenue Code §2505. This section provides a credit of up to $192,800 against lifetime and deathtime transfers and estate taxes otherwise imposed by the Code. This credit may be used all at once or over any period of years, in which case the credit is gradually reduced as it is used up. Any amount of unused credit is available as a credit against estate taxes otherwise due upon a taxpayer's death.

The unified credit of $192,800 represents the approximate tax liability on lifetime or deathtime gifts and/or a taxable estate of $600,000. Because the credit provides a dollar-for-dollar reduction of estate or gift tax owed to the IRS, an estate valued at $600,000 or less may pass free of federal tax to the beneficiaries of that estate through use of the unified credit. Even if no tax is due, an estate tax *return* indicating use of the credit must still be filed. Because each spouse has his or her own unified credit, a married couple may be able to pass $1,200,000 tax-free to their beneficiaries by effective use of their joint unified credit. This unified credit may be "used" on lifetime gifts which exceed the $10,000 annual gift exclusion allowance, which is discussed below.

☞ *STRATEGIC TIP*

It may be particularly useful to use your unified credit to gift property currently which you expect to appreciate in value in the future. This technique "removes" future appreciation from your estate (along with the earnings of the property) which can help reduce your taxable estate. Consideration was recently given to reducing the unified credit from $600,000 to $200,000, which would, of course, have the effect of raising taxes and, so, raising money for the federal government. The Revenue Reconciliation Act of 1993, however, left the $600,000 credit intact. Nevertheless, you should discuss the status of the credit with your advisors, as it is subject to change in the future. In any event, the unified credit should remain an important estate-planning tool to be used in formulating your estate plan.

Generation-Skipping Taxes

Prior to 1977, it was possible for wealthy persons to transfer their property in a manner which could avoid several generations of estate or gift tax. In the typical scenario, a wealthy person would transfer a substantial amount of money to a trust which would be invested to produce income. Under the terms of the trust, the income (and a small portion of the principal) could be used by the children, then grandchildren, then great-grandchildren, etc. of the person establishing the trust. Through this device, the only gift or estate tax due was that payable on the initial transfer of money into trust. In 1977, Congress passed a law to eliminate this tax avoidance technique and to help make sure that every generation is taxed on wealth it transfers to later generations (so that no generation tax is "skipped"). Since this "generation-skipping tax" is very complex and applies only to individuals with great wealth, we leave to others a detailed treatment of its provisions and, for now, merely call your attention to its existence.

Deferring Your Estate Tax Payments

As noted above, estate tax liability for many individuals can be large and, at times, even force the sale of a family business to raise enough money to pay this tax. In recognition of the often confiscatory effect of the estate tax, Congress added an important provision to the Internal Revenue Code which is specifically designed for family (or closely held) business owners who may be "wealthy" but are too short on "liquid wealth" to comfortably meet their estate tax obligations. Section 6166 of the Code provides that certain owners of such businesses (who qualify, among other things, based on the value of their percentage interest in a business and the number of business owners) may *defer* their estate tax payments which are attributable to their business by (1) only paying interest on the estate tax for the first five years following the former owner's death and (2) paying the estate tax itself in installments over the ensuing ten-year period.

☞ *STRATEGIC TIP*

Section 6166 may enable a financially strong family business to continue operating and, over time, to generate sufficient cash to pay the estate tax due upon an owner's death. Application of Section 6166 is extremely complex and you should discuss its possible usefulness for your planning needs with your attorney.

ESTATE PLANNING AND FORM OF BUSINESS

As discussed in chapter one, your business may be formed as a sole proprietorship, general partnership, limited partnership or corporation. Among other factors, these respective business forms may offer various advantages and disadvantages in implementing your estate plan. Some of these factors include:

Protecting Your Estate – Limited Liability

Corporations and limited partnerships, as discussed in chapter one, generally afford their shareholders or limited partners limited liability. This feature may help insulate and protect all of the other assets in your estate (personal and/or unrelated business assets) from any claim arising out of the operation of such corporation or limited partnership.

Continuity

Each of the various forms of business can, with careful planning, accommodate a smooth transition from one owner to another upon the current owner's death or retirement. Because of its indefinite life and the simplicity of reflecting its ownership in share certificates which are easily transferred, a corporation may offer some advantages.

Financing Opportunities

Unless a sole proprietor wishes to take on a partner, he can only obtain financing through a loan. Similarly, a partnership can only raise money by obtaining a loan unless it is prepared to take on a new partner or obtain additional capital contributions from existing partners. A corporation, however, offers much more flexibility in raising money because its "capital structure" may consist of common and preferred stock, including voting and nonvoting shares. While this flexibility is useful for other capital requirements (see chapter three), it can also be used to help increase the liquidity of an estate by, for example, having a business owner sell or retain only particular classes of stock in his business. Such financing opportunities make corporations an attractive form for estate planning.

Gift-Giving Flexibility

As discussed below, one important estate planning technique for family business owners is to give away up to $10,000 tax free per year to each of the owner's heirs or designated beneficiaries. This technique helps reduce the size of the owner's gross taxable estate and, thereby, reduces the estate tax which must be paid on his demise. Because it is not unusual for a business owner to have most of his wealth "locked-up" in his business, the owner may wish to give away an ownership interest in his business valued at $10,000 per year (as opposed to cash gifts of $10,000). If an interest is given in a proprietorship to reflect a $10,000 gift, the business may become a partnership and the gift recipient may have (in the absence of a partnership agreement) an equal voice in partnership operations. Similarly, if a gift of a partnership interest is given, the recipients become new partners, which may also raise management control issues and difficult tax issues relating to the value (or basis) of the partnership interests. A corporation, however, can conveniently accommodate a gift by reflecting a new issuance of shares. The owner, by using voting and nonvoting and/or common and preferred shares, can also help ensure his continuing control over business operations.

Miscellaneous

Depending on the nature of your business and personal estate planning requirements, the strategic selection of a business form can often assist you in achieving your goals. We recommend that you thoroughly review these requirements with your attorney, who may find other advantages or disadvantages with available business forms.

GENERAL ESTATE PLANNING TECHNIQUES

There are two "generic" methods for transferring your business (or interests in your business) to your heirs: giving or selling such interests. Both methods are often used in combination to provide added flexibility. Gifts are useful because your children or other heirs may not have a sufficient amount of money to buy your business outright. A sale of your business (or sales of partial interests over a number of years) to your heirs may be useful to help ensure that you or your surviving spouse receives sufficient income to sustain your lifestyle after your business has been transferred to your heirs. Your heirs may be satisfied with one or both of these methods if they are permitted to operate "their" business as they choose without having to answer to you or your surviving spouse. These methods, however, have an important drawback: They are often expensive. Gifts in excess of $10,000 per donee per year are taxable. For gift tax purposes, if property is sold for less than its fair market value, the difference between the fair value and the purchase price may be considered a gift and taxed. So, for example, if you sell one share of stock in your business for $100 when it is worth $1,000, the IRS can claim that you made a $900 gift which, subject to applicable exclusions, is taxable. Selling your business to your children may also be expensive. In order to avoid gift tax, the sale price must be at "fair market value." Depending on the value of your business, this may require your children to raise a substantial amount of money to pay for your business interests. The financing costs incurred in raising such money (see chapter three) may be too great or too onerous. In short, estate planning for many family business participants requires raising money by either the donor of a business interest (to pay gift tax) or the purchaser of a business interest (to pay the purchase price).

A number of sophisticated techniques for maximizing the efficiency of making gifts or sales have been developed which are explored in some detail below. These various techniques are frequently interrelated and, at times, may even be inconsistent with other techniques. For ease of understanding, many of the most useful estate planning techniques for family businesses are discussed below, but their relationship to each other is often important and should be carefully considered (along with other more elaborate techniques) with your professional advisors.

Estate taxes due upon a family business owner's demise can be payed from a variety of sources including use of personal savings, borrowing or insurance. All of the same sources that may help you raise money to finance your business (see chapter three) may also help your heirs finance payment of your estate taxes. These sources, however, may not be interested in this financing "opportunity" or they may be prohibitively expensive. If such is the case, the only alternative may be a forced sale of the family business to raise the necessary cash. The discussion in this chapter is designed to suggest ways to reduce or eliminate the estate tax bill so obtaining funding can be avoided or accomplished.

Plan Early

A family business owner can, of course, avoid taking steps to pass his business to his children during his lifetime, instead waiting for his demise to pass the business through his estate. This may be a very expensive option because the lifetime tax-saving strategies discussed in this chapter will have been ignored. The bigger tax bill may, in turn, force the successor owner(s) to use more of the company's resources (or borrow from a bank) to pay the bill—which typically deprives a business of resources which could be more profitably used to keep the business successful. In short, it is never too early to begin implementing your estate plan.

The "Rule Against Perpetuities"

It is not unusual for family business owners to seek to control "their" business for as long as possible. For example, they may feel financially insecure about giving up control; they may lack confidence in their heirs to handle the responsibility of running a business; or they may wish to make sure their grandchildren can operate the business one day. Whatever the reasons, the question in such circumstances usually relates to how long an owner can control the business and how such control can continue beyond the owner's life (for example, by imposing, perhaps through trusts, specific restrictions and conditions on the new owners). The infamous Rule Against Perpetuities regulates and limits the duration of such control. The rule, which is *extremely* complicated, generally provides that future interests (including ownership interest in a business) must vest unconditionally in a party within a particular time period—which can be no longer than any life in being when the future interest is created *plus* twenty-one years. Because of the rule's complexity, we leave it to others to explain its operation in proper detail. We do urge you, however, to discuss this rule with your attorney when designing your estate plan!

Gifts

Annual Exclusions Gifts. Perhaps the most time-honored estate planning technique for family business owners is to make annual gifts of stock (or other ownership interests) in the family business to the owner's children and grandchildren. Under Section 2503(b) of the Internal Revenue Code, annual gifts of up to $10,000 per beneficiary are *excluded* from gift tax. Because a spouse can consent to a further $10,000 gift to the *same* beneficiary, a husband and wife can collectively give one beneficiary up to $20,000 per year tax-free. The more of a business that is gifted away, the lower the value of the estate subject to estate tax.

To qualify for the $10,000 annual exclusion, the gift must be made with "no strings attached." Although outright gifts and gifts under the Uniform Gifts to Minors Acts qualify, the "donor" loses control of the gifted property, either immediately or when the "donee" reaches the age of eighteen or twenty-one (depending on the state where the donee resides). One solution for parents and/ or grandparents who are reluctant to lose total control over the property being gifted—or reluctant to provide "too much too soon"—to their children or grandchildren is to make the gift in trust. To satisfy the requirement that "no strings be attached" to the gift, the trust could provide that income earned by trust assets be distributed annually to the donee but the trustee controls the principal until the donee reaches an age specified by the donor. The "Crummey Trust," discussed later in this chapter, is frequently used for this purpose.

The effectiveness of an annual exclusion gifting program increases as the number of beneficiaries increase because more value can be "drawn out" of your estate. Accordingly, you should strongly consider making tax-free gifts of up to $10,000 per year to all potential beneficiaries—children, grandchildren, great-grandchildren, etc. Also, if acceptable, you may wish to consider making similar gifts to spouses of such descendants because this permits you to "enhance" the benefit of your gifting program. Such gifts can be made subject to appropriate agreements (see chapter four) that can require sale of the gifted stock back to the family in the event of a divorce.

☞ *STRATEGIC TIP*

You should strongly consider making $10,000 annual exclusion gifts of property as *early* in the year as possible. By doing so, you can remove the income and appreciation value of the property from your estate that would otherwise accrue to your estate over the course of the year.

☞ *STRATEGIC TIP*

Gifts that do not qualify for this annual exclusion may, of course, be subject to applicable gift tax. It may, nevertheless, make some planning sense for some individuals to make taxable gifts in order to help transfer business ownership from one generation to another. You may want to consider this option with your attorney.

Unified Credit Gifts. As noted above, use of the so-called unified credit permits each individual to pass up to as much as $600,000 of value to his heirs tax-free. This credit can be used at any time, in its entirety at one time or in a combination of fractional amounts over the course of a lifetime. *When* this unified credit should be used may be very important, particularly if an individual has assets — such as a family business — which are appreciating (i.e., increasing) in value. Generally, appreciating assets should be removed from an estate as early as possible to help reduce or eliminate estate tax on the appreciation amount. For example, if Owl Bookstore is worth $100,000 in 1990, $200,000 in 1991, $400,000 in 1992, and $600,000 in 1993, John Smith's stock in the business has appreciated six-fold in only four years. By using his entire unified credit in 1993, he may be able to transfer his entire ownership interest of this business to his daughter by a tax-free gift of stock. If, on the other hand, he uses his unified credit by giving $600,000 of cash to his daughter (and retains his ownership of Owl), he may have created a ticking time bomb. If, over the next ten years, Owl continues to prosper, its value may increase.

Assuming the business is worth $5,000,000 in 2003, when John dies, the estate will have to pay tax on $4,400,000 of "value" that it could have avoided by a gift of the business in 1993. Accordingly, you should strongly consider the merits of using your unified credit as early as possible to move rapidly appreciating assets from your estate to your beneficiaries.

Intrafamily Purchases and Sales

If an individual's children have sufficient (liquid) financial resources of their own, it may be possible for them to use their own resources to acquire all or part of a family business outright. For example, if John Smith's daughter, Amy, is a successful businesswoman who earns $100,000 a year, she may use some of her earnings to gradually buy out her father's interest in Owl Bookstore. The purchase price should be based on the business's fair market price in order to avoid the IRS claiming that a lower sale price was really a gift—for which gift tax must be paid.

☞ *STRATEGIC TIP*

Although this is a simple and effective technique, it generally has one important drawback: It is often unusual for children (or other lower-generation family members) to raise the money to finance such a purchase. More often than not, it is the parents (who already own the business) who have the resources in the family. If the owners give their children money to fund the purchase of the family business, the gift may be subject to gift tax. Some techniques which have been developed to help make it easier to finance such sales are discussed below.

"Holding Paper." In chapter seven, we discussed a variety of "forms" which payments for the purchase of a business could take. In addition to paying cash, one common form involves the use of a secured or unsecured promissory note—a contractual obligation to pay for the business over some period of time and which may or may not be collateralized by business or other assets owned by the buyer. This technique can work just as effectively if the buyer of your family business is your child or other beneficiary. Under applicable IRS rules, the purchase price must be based on fair market value or it can be recharacterized as a taxable gift if it is set too low. The buyer may be able to fund all or part of the note through a combination of business earnings, insurance proceeds and personal resources.

Care should be taken in using such notes because, like any other notes, they constitute an enforceable contractual agreement to pay the purchase price. If, for any reason, the buyer lacks the necessary amount of money to meet the payment obligations evidenced by the note, he will be in default and faces a collection suit from the seller. Alternatively, the seller, who may not be interested in pursuing such a suit, will be left holding a virtually worthless piece of paper which he received in exchange for his business. Finally, it is noted that replacing one asset in your estate (your business) with another asset (cash or a promissory note) may not *reduce* your estate. It may, however, (1) make your estate more liquid and, so, facilitate payment of estate taxes; and (2) avoid future appreciation of your estate if the business continues to rise in value.

"Net Gifts" of Stock. A "net gift" is a combination sale and gift transaction that is structured so that the sale proceeds received by the seller of stock in a business are sufficient to pay the gift tax that the seller must pay to reflect the taxable gift element of the transfer. For example, an individual may sell $3,000 worth of stock in his business to his child for $1,000. Thus, the seller would also be making a $2,000 gift. If the seller pays taxes at the 50 percent level, the gift tax due (one-half of $2,000) is $1,000, which could be paid from the sale proceeds. This program may help eliminate the appreciation of value in the stock from the seller's estate and is also a mechanism for "prepaying" gift and/or estate tax which might otherwise be due upon the seller's demise. You may want to discuss this program with your attorney.

Private Annuities. One useful device that permits younger family members to buy out the interests of older family members is the use of a private annuity. A private annuity is essentially a contractual agreement by the buyer(s) of the business to pay an annual amount of money to a shareholder in exchange for part or all of the shareholder's interest in the business. Basically, the fair market price for the business interest being sold is "converted" into an amount of money to be paid over the seller's lifetime on an annual basis. In order to properly establish a private annuity, the price established for the business interest being sold must be based on fair market value, and the buyer's contractual obligation to pay the annual annuity amount *cannot* be backed (or secured) by the business. You must be careful to consider these and other applicable requirements with your attorney.

☞ *STRATEGIC TIP*

Private annuities can sometimes provide unexpected (though perhaps undesired) "planning" benefits: Because a buyer's obligation to make annuity payments terminates upon the seller's death, the buyer "benefits" if the seller dies prior to his life expectancy, which helped determine the annual annuity payment amounts. Similarly, if the seller *outlives* his life expectancy, he will receive *more* (i.e., additional annuity payments) than was contemplated. In this latter event, the buyer will have effectively purchased the business interest at a premium.

Selling to Non-Family Members. In the event it is impossible, impractical, or simply undesirable to transfer a family business from a senior to junior generation, the business can be sold to nonfamily members. Such a sale may virtually eliminate an estate liquidity problem because the family will have relatively liquid assets which can be used to pay applicable estate taxes.

ESTATE FREEZES

The term "estate freeze" is a generic term for any estate planning technique which is designed to prevent an estate from increasing in value—to "freeze" the value at its current level. Although freeze devices may not necessarily reduce current assets, they can prevent these assets from increasing in future years. Freeze techniques are most useful when applied to assets that are likely to appreciate (i.e., increase) in value over the years. For example, if you can gift $10,000 either in the form of cash *or* in the form of stock in your family business, you should consider the latter gift if the business is increasing in value. If the stock does increase in value to $20,000, you have effectively doubled the value of your gift and you have helped eliminate (or "freeze") that growth out of your estate.

☞ *STRATEGIC TIP*

As the above example illustrates, estate-freezing devices can play a useful part in designing your estate plan. While these devices may limit the "growth" of your wealth, they do not, however, transfer your wealth to your beneficiaries. A program which only "freezes" your estate without also transferring your wealth with the least tax liability is usually undesirable.

Historically, many family-owned corporations implemented estate freezes by "recapitalizing" the corporation's capital structure so that senior family members would be given preferred stock and junior family members would be given common stock. These freezes were traditionally effective because much of the value of the business could simply be "transferred" by, in effect, recharacterizing the ownership interests if the business never paid dividends on its preferred stock. The junior family members would be given common stock that had "no value" but, as the business appreciated, would increase greatly in value. The Internal Revenue Code has been amended so that this once traditional form of estate freeze has now lost much of its usefulness. Currently, to be recognized by the IRS, recapitalizations of stock must be based on real (not fictional) value. Stock recapitalizations, although no longer a viable method to freeze out value that may already *exist* in an estate, may nevertheless be useful to help freeze out value that may otherwise accumulate in your estate in the *future*. You may want to discuss the possible effect of stock recapitalizations on your estate with your attorney.

TRUSTS
Although a detailed consideration of the use of trusts is beyond the scope of this book, their importance to estate planning opportunities for family business owners requires some discussion. Generally, trusts are used for a variety of reasons when a person seeks to transfer property without making an outright gift or transfer of such property. Reasons may include concerns that the donee is too young or incapable of managing his assets or a concern that, if an outright gift were made, the donee would then use the gifted property for purposes which are unsatisfactory from the donor's perspective. An individual can often transfer property, including an ownership interest in a business, to a trust in order that a "trustee" holds and manages the property for the benefit of the trust "beneficiary." While there are numerous types of trusts which are useful for different purposes, all trusts are based on a trustee's fiduciary responsibility to hold title to certain property

for the benefit of another party, the beneficiary. A trust is established by a grantor (sometimes called a "settlor"), who may or may not also be the trustee. In addition to providing for the management of assets by a fiduciary, helping create appropriate controls and restrictions on your property, estate planning with trusts can also help minimize income and estate taxes.

While trusts may be expensive to set up and then administer, they can be very useful, especially for making larger gifts and bequests. Trusts can be used to (1) postpone the donee's receipt of gifted property beyond the age of his maturity and (2) reallocate property gifted to the trust to another donee (beneficiary) in the event of certain circumstances which can be specified in the trust document (such as the death of the primary beneficiary). Accordingly, you may wish to consider these trust forms in more detail with your professional advisor. The following is a broad overview of ten of the most popular forms of trusts for family business owners.

Revocable Living Trust

A revocable living trust (or "living trust") is often touted as a means of avoiding probate (and probate fees), and to provide for management of a person's assets in the event of physical or mental disability. A revocable living trust is established by a person who retains complete power to revoke or amend any or all of the trust's terms. Because the settlor retains the power to revoke and amend the trust, all of the property held in this trust is subject to estate tax upon his death. These trusts may provide some planning flexibility, but do not minimize estate or gift taxes.

Irrevocable Living Trust

In this type of trust, the settlor has no power to alter or revoke the terms of the trust. While this obviously reduces the flexibility of this trust, it offers certain advantages. For example, assets which are contributed to the trust are *not* included in the grantor's estate (so no estate tax is due) and, if contributions to the trust are within allowable gift tax exclusions and provide the beneficiary with appropriate "withdrawal" power, gift tax can be avoided.

Crummey Trust

This type of trust contains a provision that entitles the beneficiary to withdraw a limited amount of principal and/or income from the trust during a limited time each year. This "withdrawal right" can be used to establish that new contributions to the trust qualify as a present property interest, which can qualify for the annual gift tax exclusion. If the trust is irrevocable, assets contributed by the settlor to the trust are not included in the settlor's estate and, so, estate tax on such amounts may be avoided.

Grantor Retained Income Trust ("GRIT")

A GRIT is designed to pay the grantor income generated by the trust for a period of years, with the remainder interest passing to his family members. Essentially, the grantor transfers assets to a trust which produces income. After expiration of the trust, the assets can be distributed to the trust beneficiaries, who are selected by the grantor. GRITs may produce estate tax savings because, if the grantor outlives the terms of the trust, the trust property will be excluded from his estate without any estate tax due.

Bypass Trust

A bypass trust can be used to provide an individual's surviving spouse with a lifetime interest in the trust property and, upon the surviving spouse's death, the property passes to the settlor's children or other designated beneficiaries. This trust is useful if the settlor wishes to transfer ultimate ownership of his property to someone other than his surviving spouse. A bypass trust may also be useful in helping the settlor use his $600,000 unified credit by "bypassing" $600,000 worth of assets from his spouse to be held in trust for his heirs. This technique may help ensure that the unified credit is not otherwise lost by a transfer of the entire estate to the surviving spouse through the unlimited marital deduction.

Marital Trust

A marital trust gives the grantor's surviving spouse the power to select the ultimate beneficiaries of the trust upon his or her death. Because of this power, this trust is often referred to as a "power of appointment trust." This trust may be designed to provide the surviving spouse with a right to use all or part of the income generated by the trust or to consume or transfer the trust property while alive.

Qualified Terminable Interest Property Trust ("QTIP")

This type of trust requires that income generated by the trust be distributed at least annually to the settlor's spouse. The settlor's spouse must be the only income beneficiary while alive. Upon the death of the spouse, the trust terminates and the trust property passes to the beneficiaries designated by the grantor (who are typically his children).

Irrevocable Life Insurance Trust

This type of trust is frequently used as a means for channeling life insurance benefits upon the death of the insured. Because the proceeds flow to the trust (and not to the owner's business), the settlor's estate is not augmented by the amount of insurance and, so, additional estate tax is not due. As noted above, life insurance can be useful in providing liquidity to an estate; this device helps make sure that the "cure" does not compound the problem being treated.

Charitable Remainder Trust

This type of trust permits the grantor to provide an income stream to him or herself (or designated beneficiaries) for life and then transfer the trust property to a designated charitable beneficiary. The grantor (or grantor's spouse) receives a charitable deduction for the value of the property which passes to the charity.

Charitable Lead Trust

Unlike the charitable remainder trust, which provides the grantor with an income interest and a remainder interest to charity, a charitable lead trust first provides a charity with an income interest while the remainder interest is retained by the grantor (or transferred to the grantor's children or other noncharitable beneficiaries). Among other advantages, this trust helps the grantor reduce the value of his estate by removing the value of the charitable income interest from the estate, while permitting asset retention and control and, of course, fulfillment of charitable objectives.

OWNERSHIP AGREEMENTS

As chapters four and five indicate, co-owners of a business may find it useful to enter into an agreement which describes how they will act in a variety of circumstances. These shareholder agreements can also be extremely helpful in formulating and implementing an appropriate estate plan to help safeguard the continuity of a family business. The following are several of the most frequently used forms of such agreements:

Stock Redemption Agreement

In a stock redemption agreement, the company agrees to purchase some or all of a shareholder's stock in the company. The price for the stock must be based on its fair market value. The purchase may be easier for a company with positive cash flow and retained earnings than for the shareholder's successors. Unlike private annuities, redemptions *can* be collateralized by a company's assets.

☞ *STRATEGIC TIP*

Stock that is "redeemed" by a corporation becomes "treasury stock" — that is, stock that is held in the corporation's treasury much like stock that has been authorized but not issued to any shareholder. This status may cause an unintended dilutive effect on the ownership interests in authorized *and issued* stock. For example, if John Smith owns 50 percent of stock in a company, his daughter, Amy, owns 10 percent and an unrelated investor owns 40 percent, a redemption of John's 50 percent interest will result in Amy owning only 20 percent of the company, while the outside investor now owns an 80 percent interest! Careful planning, which may include a right given to Amy to "buy back" the redeemed shares, may be necessary to avoid such consequences.

Buy-Sell Agreement

In contrast to a redemption agreement where the corporation becomes obligated to repurchase a shareholder's stock, the shareholders can agree among themselves to purchase each other's shares under certain conditions. When the shareholders (as opposed to the corporation) are obligated to make such a purchase, the contract is often called a "buy-sell" agreement. Under recent changes to the Internal Revenue Code, the buy-out price established by family members pursuant to such an agreement must reflect a fair market value. Undervalued prices can be disregarded by the IRS. This type of agreement may offer the purchaser some tax advantages (such as a "stepped-up basis" in the stock that is purchased). Disadvantages may include the personal liability on the party obligated to buy stock to satisfy his obligation to do so.

☞ *STRATEGIC TIP*

You should discuss with your advisors the merits of funding the purchase price under a buy-sell agreement with insurance. Insurance is often a satisfactory mechanism for providing the necessary liquidity, yet it must be carefully placed to avoid unnecessary income and estate taxes.

NONACTIVE HEIRS OF A FAMILY BUSINESS OWNER

One of the most difficult estate planning issues facing the owner of a family business is developing a plan which fairly provides for both heirs who are active in the business and heirs who are not. An easy solution is to provide the inactive heirs with cash or other nonbusiness assets with a value approximately equal to the value of the business interests left to the active heir. This solution, however, is often impossible to implement because, for many family business owners, the business interest comprises most of the value of the owner's estate. For this reason, there may not be a perfect "legal" solution to what is essentially a business (or financial) problem. Nevertheless, several strategies (in no particular order of importance) can be considered, including:

Attempt to Build Up Nonbusiness Assets

To the extent possible, you may be able to save and invest your earnings from the family business over the years so that the inactive heirs (who you may wish to give all such savings to) will have some inheritance — which may even be substantial.

Transfer (Restricted) Ownership Interests to Inactive Heirs

As discussed throughout this book, there is a difference between owning a business and being employed by the business.

Your active heirs may be compensated for their efforts with fair salaries, but you may wish to consider transferring stock in the business to your inactive heirs. There is a tremendous amount of flexibility you may have in making such transfers. For example, the stock you transfer could be voting or nonvoting, subject to a restrictive stock agreement, subject to a mandatory redemption agreement, etc. Such flexibility can be helpful in accommodating your family's particular needs.

"Split Dollar" Insurance

One strategy to consider is having your family business buy a so-called "split dollar" policy on the life of an owner under which the inactive heirs are the beneficiaries. The benefits paid on the death of the owner are "split" between the business (which recovers its premium costs) and the inactive heirs (who receive all of the remaining death benefit proceeds). The business is not financially impaired and the inactive heirs have received a substantial benefit.

Miscellaneous

There may be additional mechanisms that you can utilize to fairly provide for all of your heirs—not just those active in your family business. You should discuss other possible strategies with your attorney.

CONCLUSION

We hope that you have enjoyed reading our book. We also hope that you have developed a better understanding of some of the most important personal, business and legal issues you and your family business face. Although we have discussed many issues, and alluded to many others, we do not pretend that this book constitutes an exhaustive discussion of the many issues that affect, or are likely to affect, most family businesses over the course of their existence. Our primary assumption in writing this book, however, has been that a member of a family business who is sensitive to these issues will be best equipped to manage the business in a constructive and profitable fashion, and will also be better equipped to deal quickly and effectively when tensions or difficulties arise.

As we have emphasized throughout, we have not written this book as a substitute for legal advice. The law is complex, and the application of the law to specific problems facing a specific business requires careful, individualized analysis. However, we believe that the understanding we have sought to impart to you in this book will enable you to take a proactive role in the affairs of your business and in consultations with your attorney and other professional advisors. We have found over the years that our clients who have developed an understanding of the "big legal picture" are better able to make decisions appropriate to their unique circumstances than those clients who wait to react to problems as they arise without attempting to develop such an understanding.

Although the success of a family business can be measured in many ways, for most families, success is measured by reference to profitability and family harmony. We hope that this book contributes to both.

INDEX

Other Books of

Homemade Money — How to select, start, manage, market and multiply the profits of your home-based business. You'll find professional advice on legal, accounting, marketing, and tax matters — presented in no-nonsense, easy-to-understand language. *#70231/384 pages/$19.95, paperback*

Surviving the Start-Up Years in Your Own Business — Draws on the experience of successful business owners, to offer information on start-up capital, how to manage money, dealing with employees, when to expand, pricing goods and services, registration and taxes; and includes checklists, forms, charts, and more. *#70109/172 pages/$7.95, paperback*

Success, Common Sense and the Small Business — Details all the hats you must wear when starting your own business: salesperson, marketer, and office manager. Learn how to build a strong business foundation by selecting appropriate employees, consultants, partners; setting goals; creating and promoting a successful business image; and much more. *#70212/176 pages/$11.95, paperback*

Stay Home and Mind Your Own Business — Includes advice on choosing an appropriate product, service or creative business; doing market and feasibility studies; pricing and more. *#70105/280 pages/$12.95, paperback*

People, Common Sense, and the Small Business — Covers the ins and outs of finding and hiring the right people; then successfully training, motivating and supervising them. And includes guidelines for establishing a good working relationship with vendors and customers. *#70083/224 pages/ $9.95, paperback*

Export-Import: Everything You and Your Company Need to Know to Compete in World Markets — Covers every aspect of international trade, from the point of view of a U.S.-based exporter/importer — selling and shipping overseas, getting paid in U.S. dollars, and where to turn for additional help. *#70146/160 pages/$12.95, paperback*

Use the order form below (photocopy acceptable) and save when you order two or more books!

☐ **Yes!**

Book #   Price

Credit Card O

*Please add $3
shipping is FR

Check enclo
Acct # ____
Name ____
Address ____
City ____

3131

GAYLORD S